Baby Play & Learn

Penny Warner

 **Meadowbrook Press**

Distributed by Simon & Schuster
New York

Library of Congress Cataloging-in-Publication Data
Warner, Penny.
    Baby play & learn/Penny Warner.
       p. cm.
    Includes index.
    ISBN 0-88166-328-X (Meadowbrook)—ISBN 0-671-31655-9 (Simon & Schuster)
    1. Infants—Development. 2. Play. 3. Educational games. 4. Child rearing.
  I. Title. II. Title: Baby play and learn.
  HQ774.W36   1999
  305.232—dc21   98-56097
                                           CIP

Editor: Liya Lev Oertel
Production Manager: Joe Gagne
Production Assistant: Danielle White
Illustrations: Jack Lindstrom

Published by Meadowbrook Press, 5451 Smetana Drive, Minnetonka, MN 55343

BOOK TRADE DISTRIBUTION by Simon & Schuster, a division of Simon and Schuster, Inc., 1230 Avenue of the Americas, New York, NY 10020

03   10 9 8 7 6

Printed in the United States of America

TABLE OF CONTENTS

INTRODUCTION

Welcome to *Baby Play & Learn*. The fun and games are about to begin!
Your baby's most rapid period of growth and development takes place between
the years from birth to three. Your baby grows

- *physically*—by practicing both fine and gross motor skills;
- *cognitively*—by increasing thinking and problem-solving skills;
- *verbally*—by acquiring receptive and expressive communication;
- *psychologically*—by discovering more about self-identity;
- *socially*—by learning how to interact with others;
- *emotionally*—by mastering the expression of emotions.

At no other time, aside from prenatal development, does your baby grow,
change, and learn more rapidly than during these early years. By providing a stimulating environment, you—as a parent, teacher, or caregiver—can help your baby
reach his developmental potential during this critical time.

Keep the following three things in mind:

1. Your baby learns primarily through play.
2. The best plaything for your baby is you.
3. Have fun with your baby!

Since you are the best plaything for your baby, you've got most of the equipment right on hand—your face, your hands, and your body. All you need are a few
stimulating ideas, some creative materials, and time to enjoy the fun.

Baby Play & Learn offers 160 specific games and activities for hours of developmental challenges and rewards. Each game and activity is based on the recom-
mendations of a number of current child development experts. After much
research in the area of babies' learning and growth, authorities have found lots of
ways to help kids reach their full potential—and have a good time along the way.
As a child development instructor for twenty years, I know how much parents
enjoy playing with their babies—all they want is more ideas for fun and games!

In this book you will find

- Recommended ages for each game and activity.
- A list of easy-to-find materials needed for each game and activity.
- Step-by-step instructions for each game and activity.
- Variations for added fun and enhanced learning.
- Safety tips to ensure your baby doesn't get hurt while playing.
- A list of skills your baby learns through play.

Following are a few important points to keep in mind as you enjoy your time with your baby:

- ***Babies learn through their senses.*** Provide lots of stimulating materials for your baby to look at, listen to, taste, touch, and smell. Keep in mind—the best toy for your baby is one that stimulates all five senses—and that's you!

- ***Babies respond to a rich environment.*** That doesn't mean that you have to provide your baby with hundreds of toys. You should, however, select developmentally appropriate toys, offer your baby a variety from which to choose, and let your baby have plenty of time to play. Remember, simpler is better. The simpler the toy, the more complex the play.

- ***Babies learn from imitation.*** Babies like to do what everyone else does. You play the game first, and your baby will learn from you. Be sure to use lots of body language and facial expression while you demonstrate the game, activity, or toy. Better yet, let an older child be a role model for your baby to imitate. Babies love to play with other kids.

- ***Babies learn from different kinds of play***. Games and activities help babies better understand their feelings, their fears, and their world. Babies like to play

  —*alone,* so they can set the pace, solve their own problems, and make their own choices.
  —*with others,* so they can observe other types of play, learn new ways of exploring, and become social in their play.
  —*quietly,* with fingers, toes, books, music, finger toys, and language.
  —*actively,* using their arms and legs to move, throw, bounce, and dance.
  —*make-believe,* when they become monsters, doggies, mommies, daddies, superheroes, and cartoon characters. Another variation of make-believe play is when babies act out home life, daycare, preschool, hospital visits, birthday parties, holidays, or even funerals.

- ***Babies learn from repetition.*** Babies love to play games over and over and over. Start with a simple task, make it fun, then make it more challenging over time, as your baby becomes better able to process information, use his body, and interact with others. Your baby's favorite word will soon be "Again!"

- ***Babies develop through experience.*** Although babies begin playing and learning by watching others, being onlookers won't satisfy them for long. Your baby wants to be a doer. Get your baby involved with the environment at every opportunity. No baby is too young to take the most basic steps toward playing and learning. Let your baby try, and offer your help only when needed.

- **Babies get smarter by problem solving.** Set up simple skill-building tasks for your baby to solve, and increase the challenge as your baby develops. Keep the challenges easy to solve, so your baby doesn't become frustrated and stop trying, yet challenging enough to keep your baby entertained and interested. Help your baby build small steps of success on the way to solutions.

- **Babies learn through language.** Talk to your baby while you play, and explain what you're doing and why. Babies often understand more than we think, and explaining the purpose or directions of a game, activity, or toy is a good habit. Babies enjoy language games, so make language a part of your play.

- **Babies proceed at their own pace.** Don't rush playtime or overwhelm your baby with too many options at a time. And don't try to push too high a level of development if your baby isn't ready. Observe as your baby plays to familiarize yourself with his internal pace, then be ready to add more challenges as needed.

- **Babies are competent when they feel confident.** Give your baby lots of praise and encouragement while you play, and set your baby up for success instead of failure. Help your baby find new ways to play, solve problems, make discoveries, and learn. And have a good time!

Most of all, your baby wants to play with you. The learning aspect of play is just a bonus. So turn the page, and let the fun with your baby begin! It's Play Time!

BiRTH TO THREE MONTHS

Experts used to think your baby was a helpless being at birth. They said a baby couldn't see, hear, or think. But studies have proven that your baby can see, hear, and even learn long before she's born; your baby's growth in the uterus is the most rapid period of your baby's development.

The period from birth to three months is the second most rapid period of development. As soon as your baby is born, learning takes rapid leaps in all areas of development—cognitive or thinking skills, physical growth and motor control, and personality development, including emotional expression, self-awareness, and social skills. To make the most of this valuable period, begin at birth to enhance your baby's development in all areas.

Cognition begins immediately, as your baby tries to figure out her new world and make sense of her environment. Although, on average, your baby takes in language for twelve months before she says her first word, by the time she does, she already has a fifty-word vocabulary. The wheels turn constantly as your baby rapidly improves her thinking skills. Before you know it, she'll be solving her own problems, asking unanswerable questions, and learning how to get what she wants. This section includes lots of games for you to play with your baby to enhance cognitive development.

As your baby begins to physically develop, you'll see changes in motor control, from the first attempts at eye/hand coordination (with uncoordinated swipes at the air), to the ability to walk, run, climb, ride, even ski! The steps are small and nearly invisible along the way, but you and your baby can practice with a variety of fun games provided in this section.

Your baby's psychological and social skills are also making swift gains, from that first moment of eye contact, to the ability to express herself emotionally, acquire new social relationships, and understand her uniqueness. Play further develops these personality skills, helping your baby become well-balanced psychologically, socially, and emotionally.

What are you waiting for? Take advantage of every moment of these first three months. Your baby grows quickly!

ALL GONE!

Since your baby is new on the planet, he spends much of his time trying to figure out his environment. Help him by playing a game of All Gone!

Materials:
- Soft, colorful toys
- Box or bucket
- Blanket, towel, or cloth

Learning Skills:	• Anticipation of events • Cognitive/thinking skills • Object permanence and stability

What to Do:

1. Collect several soft, colorful toys, and place them in a box or bucket, out of sight.

2. Seat your baby comfortably in his infant seat and sit opposite him.

3. Bring one toy out of the box and show it to your baby. Hold the toy close to your face and talk to your baby, to attract his attention.

4. While your baby is watching, cover the toy with a cloth.

5. Say to your baby, "All gone!"

6. Wait a few seconds, then uncover the toy and happily announce, "Here it is!"

7. Repeat with different toys.

Variation: After you hide the toy under a cloth several times, place the toy out of sight. Watch your baby's reaction as he tries to figure out what happened; then bring the toy out into view again. Try various hiding places to keep your baby intrigued.

Safety: If your baby gets upset at the toy's disappearance, hide the toy slowly to show him what you're doing. Don't leave the toy covered for too long.

BABY BALL

Everybody needs exercise—even your newborn baby! Baby Ball is a fun way to get your baby's circulation going, limber up muscles, increase flexibility, and help your baby learn to control her body movements.

Materials:
- Large ball, approximately 2 to 3 feet in diameter (available at toy, sporting goods, and teacher supply stores)
- Large section of carpeted floor

Learning Skills:	• Motor control and flexibility • Spatial relationships • Trust

What to Do:

1. Dress your baby only in a diaper, so her body will grip the surface of the ball without slipping.

2. Set a ball in the middle of the room on a carpeted surface.

3. Sit on the floor facing the ball. Stand your baby on the opposite side of the ball, facing you. Hold her arms to balance her.

4. Roll your baby up onto the ball, carefully holding her so she doesn't slip or fall.

5. Roll your baby around the ball, forward and backward, and side to side.

6. Experiment with the ball and try different exercises.

Variation: Deflate the ball a little. If you don't have a ball, use a couch pillow or cushion.

Safety: Make sure you hold your baby securely at all times, so she doesn't fall or roll off the ball. To ensure trust between you and your baby, move the ball and your baby slowly.

BABY MASSAGE

Your baby begins to respond to touch immediately after birth. The first welcome your baby receives is the tactile comfort of your touch as you hold him. Provide your baby with a Baby Massage so he can delight in the pleasure of your soothing hands.

Materials:
- Blanket or towel
- Baby lotion

Learning Skills:	• Body awareness
	• Enhanced sense of touch
	• Social interaction

What to Do:

1. Spread a blanket or a towel on a soft carpet.

2. Place your naked baby on the blanket, on his tummy.

3. Pour a little baby oil into your hands and rub your hands together to warm up the oil.

4. Gently massage your baby from his neck to his shoulders, down his arms to his hands, down his back to his buttocks, down his legs, and to his feet. Use a gentle touch, not too firm and not too light.

5. Turn your baby over on his back and repeat, using more oil.

Variation: Give your baby a foot or hand massage any time, while nursing, bathing, or sitting at the park; oil is not necessary.

Safety: Use a soft touch so you don't cause any rug burns! Be sure your baby isn't allergic to the oils or lotions you use. Avoid touching your baby's face so the oils don't get into your baby's eyes.

BUBBLE BATH

Bath time is fun for most babies, although some don't seem to like the water. But no matter what kind of reaction you get from your baby, you can make bath time more fun by adding a few baby bubbles while you wash.

Materials:
- Soft washcloth
- Plastic baby tub
- Baby bubble bath
- Towel

Learning Skills:	• Body awareness • Language development • Listening skills • Sensory stimulation

What to Do:
1. Lay a washcloth on the bottom of your baby's plastic tub to help keep your baby from sliding around.

2. Fill the tub with warm water and add a small amount of baby bubble bath solution.

3. Place your baby into the tub, holding her securely at all times to gain her trust.

4. Sit your baby up so she can safely enjoy the bubbles and splash the water if she wants.

5. Wash your baby's body parts while singing "This Is the Way We Wash":

> *This is the way we wash our face,*
> *Wash our face, wash our face.*
> *This is the way we wash our face,*
> *Baby (name) and Mommy.*

Continue the song with "...clean our neck," "...rub our chest," "...scrub our back," "...bathe our arms," "...soap our legs," "...tidy our toes," and so on.

Variation: Get into the bath with your baby and wash yourselves together. Put some toys into the tub, or use a washcloth in the shape of an animal or a puppet.

Safety: Follow these two rules to make sure your baby enjoys the bath:
- Be certain that your baby feels secure at all times—don't let her slip or dunk under the water.
- Make sure the water is always warm—not too hot and not too cold.

BUZZY BEE

From birth, your baby starts to learn through his senses. This game will help your baby develop his ability to locate sound, which leads to better head control and general motor movement.

Materials:
- Soft blanket
- Your mouth
- Your finger

Learning Skills:	• Head and neck control • Location of sound and touch • Motor movement and control • Social interaction

What to Do:

1. Place your baby on his back on a soft blanket.

2. Sit near your baby so he can hear you clearly.

3. Make a sound imitating a buzzing bee as you move your finger close to your baby's body.

4. After a few seconds, touch your baby with your finger and say, "Buzzy bee!"

5. Repeat, landing on different parts of your baby's body.

Variation: Move your head to follow your finger, so your baby can track the sound. Vary the pitch of the buzzing sound, from high to low, to keep the sound interesting. Turn your baby over on his tummy and play again. This time he won't be able to see your finger move and will have to wait for the Buzzy Bee surprise!

"BUZZZZ!"

Safety: Touch your baby softly and don't make the sound too loud. If your baby startles, slow down the game.

EYE WINKER

The face is a good place to start teaching your baby about body parts. Play a game of Eye Winker to help your baby distinguish her nose from her mouth from her eyes—and teach her what each does!

Materials:
- Your baby's face
- Your finger

Learning Skills:	• Recognition of facial features • Sensory enjoyment—touch • Social interaction • Understanding of body parts

What to Do:
1. Hold your baby on your lap, facing you.

2. Say or sing the following chant while touching the coordinating body parts:

> *Eye winker* (gently touch eyelid)
> *Lid blinker* (gently touch other eyelid)
> *Nose smeller* (gently touch tip of nose)
> *Mouth eater* (gently touch bottom lip)
> *Chin chopper* (gently pull down chin)
> *Neck drinker* (gently run finger down neck)
> *Tummy tickler* (gently run finger down to tummy, gently tickle)

3. Repeat several times.

Variation: After you've played Eye Winker a few times, try a round of Chin Chopper:

Knock on the door (gently knock on your baby's forehead)
Peep in (gently lift one of your baby's eyelids)
Open the latch (gently press your baby's nose up)
And walk in (gently walk two fingers on your baby's bottom lip)
Chin chopper, chin chopper, chin chopper, chin (gently open and close your baby's jaw)

Safety: Be sure your touch is gentle or the game won't be pleasant for your baby!

FiNGER FACE

From birth, your baby prefers to look at a human face above all other objects. Something about the eyes, nose, and mouth attracts your baby's attention. Finger Face is based on that fascination.

Materials:
- Knit glove
- Scissors
- Your hand
- Colorful felt-tip pens

Learning Skills:	• Ability to focus
	• Recognition of faces
	• Social interaction

What to Do:

1. Cut the fingers off a knit glove.

2. Using felt-tip pens, draw a face in the middle of the glove's palm. Make the eyes and mouth large, bright, and colorful.

3. Slip the glove onto your hand.

4. Hold your baby in your lap and turn the glove face toward him.

5. Now wiggle your fingers and move the face around slowly so your baby can enjoy his new Finger Face friend, who can help you sing songs, tell stories, or just chat.

Variation: Make Finger Face three dimensional. Sew or glue-gun wiggly eyes to the middle of the glove, make a mouth from red felt, and add a pom-pom nose in the center.

Safety: If your baby gets ahold of the Finger Face, he will probably put it right into his mouth, so make sure the eyes, mouth, and nose are securely attached.

FOOTSY FUN

Your baby begins learning to control her arms and legs from the moment she is born, but reflexes and lack of coordination seem to get in the way. Work on motor control with a game of Footsy Fun.

Materials:
- Small, colorful booties
- Little bells, lightweight noisemakers, or small, soft, colorful toys
- Needle and thread
- Soft blanket
- Baby's feet

Learning Skills:	• Eye/hand and eye/foot coordination • Motor control • Problem solving • Visual tracking

What to Do:

1. Buy some small booties that are especially colorful—primary (red, blue, and yellow) or rainbow colors are best.

2. Securely sew little bells, noisemakers, or small, soft, colorful toys to the tops of the booties.

3. Lay your baby on her back on a soft blanket and slip the booties onto her feet.

4. Watch your baby enjoy her new Footsy Fun playthings.

Variation: Attach noisemakers or small toys to tiny mittens instead of booties, and place them on your baby's hands.

Safety: Be sure all items are tightly secured to the booties or mittens, and check them regularly for signs of loosening. Don't attach any sharp objects that might hurt your baby if she tries to bring them to her mouth. Watch your baby at all times.

GOTCHA GLOVE

Your baby likes surprises—as long as they're fun and not frightening! You can begin playing the universally exciting game of Gotcha with this added attraction—the Gotcha Glove!

Materials:
- Soft garden glove
- Small, soft toy animals (such as Beanie Babies), about the same size as the glove
- Needle and thread
- Soft blanket or infant seat

Learning Skills:	• Anticipation of events • Emotional expression • Social interaction • Trust

What to Do:

1. Sew a small soft toy to the back of the glove, so the toy sits on the back of your hand when the glove is worn.

2. Place your baby on his back on a soft blanket or in an infant seat.

3. Slip on the Gotcha Glove.

4. Wiggle your fingers and move the glove around, so your baby can see the animal sitting on top.

5. Make animal noises as you move the glove, to attract your baby's attention.

"GOTCHA!"

6. All of a sudden, place your gloved hand on your baby's tummy, leg, arm, or other body part, and say, "Gotcha!" with a big smile.

7. Give that body part a little tickle or wiggle, then play again.

Variation: Make two gloves, one for each hand, for added fun. Attach strips of Velcro to the glove and to several toy animals. This way you can change the animals from time to time to keep the game interesting.

Safety: If your baby gets scared, slow down your movement and talk softly. Be sure to keep smiling as you play.

HANDY CLAP

Developing eye/hand coordination takes time, but if you watch your baby carefully, you'll see her beginning attempts to control those tiny hands. Fun fingerplays can help your baby work on motor skills.

Materials:
- Soft blanket or an infant seat
- Fingerplays, songs, and rhymes
- Your hands and baby's hands

Learning Skills:	• Eye/hand coordination • Motor control • Social interaction

What to Do:

1. Lay your baby on a soft blanket or sit her upright in her infant seat, and sit close by so she can see you.

2. Sing or chant songs and rhymes while you play with your baby's hands and fingers. Try one of the following Handy Clap games:

Pat-A-Cake

Pat-a-cake, pat-a-cake, baker's man, (clap your baby's hands)
Bake me a cake as fast as you can; (repeat clapping)
Roll it (roll baby's hands) and pat it; (pat baby's hands)
Mark it with a B. (draw a B in the middle of baby's hand)
Put it in the oven for baby and me. (gently poke baby in the tummy)

If You're Happy

If you're happy and you know it, clap your hands. (clap baby's hands)
If you're happy and you know it, clap your hands. (clap baby's hands)
If you're happy and you know it, then your hands will surely show it.
If you're happy and you know it, clap your hands. (clap baby's hands)

Whoops! Johnny!

(Spread your baby's fingers open.) *Johnny* (touch baby finger tip), *Johnny* (touch next fingertip), *Johnny* (touch next fingertip), *Johnny* (touch next fingertip), *Whoops! Johnny!* (slide your finger down in between the forefinger and the thumb, then repeat going backwards) *Johnny. Whoops! Johnny! Johnny, Johnny, Johnny.*

Variation: Try these games on baby's feet instead of hands. Use your baby's name when appropriate.

Safety: Hold and move your baby's hands gently as you play.

HAPPY FEET

One of your baby's favorite toys is his feet! They're soft and wiggly, and close at hand. And they feel funny when they're touched! Have fun with Happy Feet as you combine nursery rhymes with toe touching.

Materials:
- Soft blanket
- Words to songs and nursery rhymes
- Your fingers and your baby's toes

Learning Skills:
- Body awareness
- Enjoyment of senses
- Language development
- Motor control
- Social interaction

What to Do:

1. Choose a favorite nursery rhyme that can be played with your baby's feet and toes.

2. Lay your baby on a soft blanket and kneel beside him so you can reach his feet.

3. Play one of the following Happy Feet games:

This Little Piggy
This little piggy went to market, (wiggle the big toe)
This little piggy stayed home, (wiggle the second toe)
This little piggy had roast beef, (wiggle the third toe)
This little piggy had none, (wiggle the fourth toe)
And this little piggy cried, "Wee, wee, wee!" all the way home! (wiggle the baby toe)

Gobble Gobble
Wee wiggle, (wiggle baby toe)
Two tickle, (wiggle next toe)
Three giggle, (wiggle next toe)
Four sniggle, (wiggle next toe)
Five—gobble! (pretend to gobble up your baby's foot)

Pitty Pat Pony
Pitty pat pony, (pat the soles of your baby's feet)
Look at her toes. (hold baby's feet and wiggle them)
Here a nail, there a nail, (poke the bottom of baby's feet)
Gid-up and go! (pat the soles of your baby's feet again)

Variation: Play the game using hands instead of feet.

Safety: Don't tickle your baby too much. As you probably know from personal experience, excessive tickling becomes uncomfortable.

MAGIC MIRROR

At first your baby will be curious about this new stranger she sees, but over time she will delight in seeing herself in that fascinating object called a mirror!

Materials:
- Portable, full-length mirror, if possible
- Props, such as hats, cloths, dolls

Learning Skills:	• Enhanced self-esteem • Learning body parts • Recognition of self-image • Understanding of environment

What to Do:

1. Set a full-length mirror against a wall.

2. Hold your baby in your lap close to the mirror.

3. Let your baby touch the mirror and examine its properties.

4. Interact with the mirror by waving, making faces, touching it, turning your head, and so on.

5. Use props: place a hat on your head or your baby's head, cover your baby's head with a cloth, or introduce a doll.

6. End the Magic Mirror fun by pointing out all of your baby's body parts in the mirror.

Variation: Set a nonbreakable of safety mirror flat on a soft blanket on the floor, and place your baby on top of it. Let her enjoy the view as she lifts her head, hands, and legs. Peek into the mirror so your baby can see you, too.

Safety: Make sure the mirror is propped securely against the wall, so it doesn't fall on your baby. If possible, use a nonbreakable or safety mirror.

MOUTH MUSIC

Bet you didn't know you had a whole music machine right in your mouth! Your baby loves to hear a variety noises, and your mouth is just the instrument necessary to make a perfect symphony.

Materials:
• Your mouth, tongue, teeth, and lips

Learning Skills:	• Sound discrimination • Sound imitation and language development • Sound location

What to Do:
1. Hold your baby in your lap, facing you, so he can see your face clearly.

2. Begin making noises with your mouth, such as

   • Kissing and smooching
   • Clicking your tongue
   • Making raspberries with your tongue
   • Blowing your lips like a motorboat
   • Growling, squealing, gurgling, and cooing
   • Whistling, singing, humming
   • Making animal sounds, such as a duck, dog, cat, horse, cow, pig, chicken, rooster, monkey, snake, bird, donkey, or wolf

Variation: Use a few props to enhance your Mouth Music. Try a kazoo, a harmonica, a toy horn, a homemade megaphone (a toilet paper roll), or a blade of grass between your thumbs.

Safety: If you use any instruments, make sure they are safe for your baby to try. Don't make noises too loud, or they could damage your baby's hearing. If a noise disturbs your baby, don't repeat it.

MUSICAL MOMENTS

Although your baby can hear while inside the womb, the sounds are distant and muffled. After she's born, sound becomes a source of unexplained fascination. Here's a way to enhance her listening skills!

Materials:
- Portable cassette tape recorder and blank tapes
- Variety of sounds
- Soft blanket or an infant seat

Learning Skills:	• Sound differentiation • Sound identification • Sound location

What to Do:

1. Use a portable cassette tape recorder to record several minutes of a variety of sounds. Include familiar noises, such as the bark of your dog, the sound of daddy coming home from work, the doorbell and telephone, the musical windup toy in the crib, and other sound-making toys. In addition, include some unusual sounds, such as commercial jingles, cooking sounds, animal noises, music, and mouth noises.

2. Lay your baby on a soft blanket or prop her up in an infant seat. Keep all extra sounds to a minimum.

3. Turn on the cassette player and play the recordings for your baby.

4. Watch her reaction as each new sound is played, then identify the sounds for her, using simple words.

Variation: Tape-record voices. Begin with your voice, chanting a rhyme or singing a song, then include other familiar voices, such as dad, siblings, relatives, and friends. Include a few unfamiliar voices, or disguise your voice from time to time, for variety.

Safety: If your baby seems frightened by the sounds, turn down the recorder's volume and reassure your baby by making the sounds with your mouth.

15

PEEKABOO

A simple game of Peekaboo can teach your baby many skills, such as the concept of object permanence, as you disappear and reappear!

Materials:
- Your face
- Handkerchief, washcloth, or other small cloth

Learning Skills:	• Anticipation of events • Cause and effect • Cognitive/thinking skills • Emotional expression • Object permanence • Social interaction

What to Do:
1. Hold your baby on your lap, facing you.

2. Talk to your baby, smile, or make a face to attract his attention.

3. Once you have your baby's attention, cover your head and face with the handkerchief so he can't see you.

4. After a few seconds, remove the cloth and, with a big smile on your face, say, "Peekaboo!"

5. Repeat several times.

Variation: Instead of covering your face, cover your baby's face. After a few seconds remove the cloth and say, "Peekaboo!"—or let the baby remove the cloth himself.
If you like, cover a doll instead of yourself or your baby, so you can enjoy the game together. For a higher level of development, play the game in front of a mirror, so your baby can look at lots of faces.

Safety: Use a light cloth to place over your baby's head, so he won't be frightened or have trouble breathing. Don't leave the cloth on his face for long. Repeat the game over and over; don't confuse your baby by changing the game until he is older and can understand the basics.

SHOOTING STARS

In the early months, your baby enjoys simply watching her world. Lights, colors, and movement provide hours of sensory enjoyment. This is the perfect time to introduce her to the exciting game of Shooting Stars.

Materials:
- Soft blanket
- Colorful pom-poms in different sizes
- Chair

Learning Skills:	• Anticipation of events • Eye/hand coordination • Social interaction • Visual tracking and acuity

What to Do:

1. Place your baby on a soft blanket, on her back.

2. Set a chair near your baby, so you can lean over her while you're sitting down.

3. Hold a large pom-pom over your baby's tummy, drawing attention to it with your voice.

4. After you have your baby's attention, say, "Here comes the Shooting Star," then drop the pom-pom onto your baby's tummy.

5. Give your baby a big smile so she knows you're having fun.

6. Repeat the game, dropping a smaller pom-pom onto your baby's tummy.

Variation: Instead of using pom-poms, collect light, colorful objects from around the house to use as shooting stars—soft, dry sponge shapes, feathers, paper balls, small fabric scraps, small, soft toys, and so on.

Safety: Make sure all objects are light-weight and soft, so your baby doesn't get hurt. If the game scares her, don't let the object fall. Always move objects slowly toward your baby's tummy, never her face. Keep smiling as you play, to teach your baby a sense of fun.

STiCKER FACE

Your baby's visual skills are surprisingly well-developed at birth. He can make eye contact immediately after birth, and by three months he prefers bright colors, strong contrasts, and visual surprises.

Materials:
• Your face
• Brightly colored stickers or dots

Learning Skills:	• Eye/hand coordination
	• Focusing
	• Locating objects visually

What to Do:

1. Sit in a comfortable chair with your knees up. Place your baby on your lap, facing you, with his head and body supported by your legs.

2. Let your baby have a good look at your face for a few moments while you talk with him and make funny faces.

3. Place a colorful sticker somewhere on your face—your cheek, forehead, chin, nose—and watch your baby's reaction.

4. After a few moments, move the sticker somewhere else on your face, and watch your baby find the new spot.

5. For fun, place a sticker on your tongue, then stick out your tongue and show your baby the surprise sticker. (Just don't swallow it accidentally!)

6. Place stickers on your eyelids, then close your eyes so baby can see them.

7. Place stickers on both cheeks, cover your cheeks with your hands, then play "peeka-boo" and reveal the hidden stickers.

Variation: Place stickers on both sides of your baby's hands, and watch his reaction as he discovers the colorful spots. See if he tries to find the spots by adjusting his hands. This is the beginning of self-awareness.

Safety: Be sure your baby doesn't put the stickers in his mouth and swallow them.

TOOTSIE ROLL

Your baby needs months to gain full control of her body movements, but you can assist her during those early weeks with a game of Tootsie Roll. By four to six months your baby will have mastered the rollover!

Materials:
- Soft blanket or towel
- Soft floor surface

Learning Skills:	• Directionality • Locomotion • Motor control

What to Do:

1. Place a soft blanket or towel on a soft surface.

2. Lay your baby down on the blanket, on her tummy.

3. Pick up one side of the blanket and slowly raise it, causing your baby to tilt to the side.

4. Continue to slowly roll your baby over, talking to her as you go, and using a hand to spot or guide her as she turns.

5. When your baby turns over, show your delight.

6. Repeat until your baby is tired of playing.

Variation: Instead of using a blanket or towel, use your hands. Try tucking one arm at your baby's side to make the turn easier.

Safety: Be sure to move slowly and keep a hand on your baby so she doesn't roll too fast and get hurt.

TUMMY TALK

Your baby begins learning speech and language long before he utters his first word. Besides talking to your baby, try a little Tummy Talk. It makes speech and language a sensory experience!

Materials:
- Your mouth
- Soft blanket

Learning Skills:	• Body awareness • Language development • Sensory-motor exploration • Social interaction

What to Do:
1. Remove your baby's clothes (diaper optional) and place him on a blanket, on his back.

2. Kneel down beside your baby, chat for a moment, and gently rub his tummy.

3. Now it's time for Tummy Talk. Press your face and lips onto your baby's tummy, and talk, sing, recite a nursery rhyme, or just make up funny words. Vary the pitch and loudness of your voice as you speak.

4. Add a few kisses each time you finish your words.

5. Sit up and smile at your baby after each Tummy Talk. Your baby should be giggling while you play and anticipating the next ticklish chat.

Variation: Instead of talking, make mouth noises against your baby's tummy, such as raspberries, motorboats, clicks, puffs and blows, tongue tickles, and so on.

Safety: Don't speak too loudly; you don't want to startle your baby. And if you play this game with a naked baby, keep a diaper nearby, in case of a sudden tinkle!

WiGGLE WORM

When your baby's feet press against a solid surface, she stretches out her legs. This is called the "walking reflex." Use this reflex to help your baby practice for crawling.

Materials:
- Soft, nonslippery floor surface
- Colorful toy

Learning Skills:	• Cause and effect • Motor control • Precrawling exercise

What to Do:

1. Place your baby on a soft floor, on her tummy.

2. Place a colorful toy a few inches from your baby's head and call her attention to it.

3. Sit behind your baby, with your legs or hands pressed against her feet. Your baby will push against the pressure, causing her to propel a few inches forward, toward the toy.

4. Keep moving the toy and pushing against your baby's feet until she has inched forward and covered some ground.

Variation: Place a board or other strong surface against your baby's feet.

Safety: Be careful not to move your baby too fast. Don't let her get too close to the toy, or she may hit her head against it.

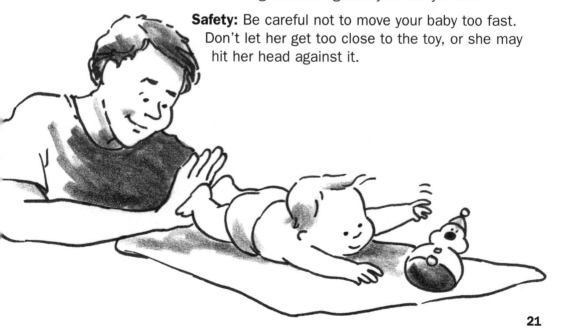

THREE MONTHS TO SiX MONTHS

At this stage of development, your baby is learning through his five senses. When your baby is born, his strongest senses are hearing and smell. He can recognize his mother's voice and, soon after, his father's. He can also distinguish various familiar sounds, such as dad's keys in the door, the dog barking, and the sound of the doorbell. He recognizes his mother by smell, and often won't take a bottle from anyone who doesn't smell like her!

Your baby's sense of touch also develops rapidly. From birth he enjoys being held and massaged, and makes rapid gains in all areas of development just by being carried and physically touched. Luckily, your baby doesn't have a long memory of pain, so if you accidentally stick him with a diaper pin, he'll forgive you quickly.

Vision and taste are two of the slower developing senses. Your baby has about 20/200 vision early in life, but by one year of age, he can see with 20/20 vision. You baby likes to look at interesting things, and he prefers faces over designs, and baby faces over adult faces. At birth, your baby can also track your finger, if you hold it ten inches from his face. By the time your baby is three months, he can see things at greater distances.

Your baby will put just about anything in his mouth—not so much for taste as for oral exploration. He learns by putting an object in his mouth and exploring it with his tongue and lips. Just by using his mouth, your baby can tell if an object is hot or cold, rough or smooth, soft or hard, big or little. But he's not ready for the taste of baby food until the end of this period, at about age six months. So let your baby use his mouth to learn and to drink mother's milk or formula, and save the jars of baby food for a few more weeks.

Help your baby develop his five senses by playing the games in this section.

BABY'S NAME SONG

You can sing Baby's Name Song any time of day—or in the middle of the night, when your baby wakes up and needs help going back to sleep. And don't worry, this activity does not require any singing talent!

Materials:
- Your voice
- Repertoire of familiar songs

Learning Skills:	• Language development • Listening skills • Social interaction

What to Do:

1. Make sure your baby is comfortable and within hearing distance—she can be lying down or sitting up on your lap or in a car seat, but facing you is best, so she can watch your face.

2. Choose a favorite familiar song, such as "Rock-A-Bye Baby," and sing the tune with personalized lyrics for your baby. For example, instead of singing "Rock-A-Bye Baby," substitute your baby's name for the word "baby."

3. Include your baby's name as often as possible in each song.

4. If you like, try "(Yankee Doodle) Came to Town," "(Mares) Eat Oats and Does Eat Oats," and "Round and Round (the Mountain) Like a Teddy Bear," substituting your baby's name for the words in parentheses.

Variation: Include information about your family, your pets, your baby's toys, and so on, to keep your baby entertained and to expand your baby's receptive vocabulary.

Safety: Try not to sing off-key. You might damage your baby's appreciation of music for life! (Just kidding!)

BABY ON THE BUS

It's time for a baby workout, set to the tune of "Wheels on the Bus." These exercises will help keep your baby in shape. He's never too young to start!

Materials:
- Soft blanket or towel on a soft surface
- Your voice

Learning Skills:	• Language development • Motor movement and control • Physical exercise

What to Do:

1. Lay your baby on a blanket or towel, on his back.

2. Remove his clothes—diaper is optional.

3. Sing the following song, moving the assigned body part on your baby as you sing.

Wheels on the Bus
(Bicycle your baby's legs as you sing the first four lines.)
The wheels on the bus go round and round,
Round and round, round and round,
The wheels on the bus go round and round,
All through the town.
The people on the bus go up and down.
(lift your baby's arms up and down)
The wipers on the bus go back and forth.
(roll baby from side to side)
The horn on the bus goes beep, beep, beep.
(touch your baby's nose)

Variation: Add more verses to the song, making them up as you go along, and adding more body parts.

Safety: Be gentle with your baby's movements.

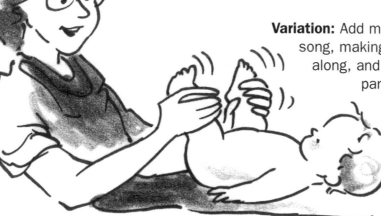

BOAT RIDE

Here's an exciting game to play with your baby as she becomes sturdier and wants to become more mobile. Give her a Boat Ride around the house, so she can see a whole new world.

Materials:
- 2 small, soft blankets or large towels
- Large, unobstructed floor surface

Learning Skills:	• Balance • Exploration • Visual stimulation

What to Do:

1. Spread soft blankets or towels on a soft surface, one on top of the other, for padded double thickness.

2. Place your baby on her back on the blankets.

3. Grasp one end of the blankets and slowly pull your baby around the room.

4. Talk about some of the things you see as you move from place to place.

Variation: Place your baby on her tummy for a different perspective. Prop up her chest with a small pillow or soft toy for extra leverage and comfort.

Safety: If your baby lies on her back, provide extra padding for her head. Move the blankets very slowly, and watch for bumps and hazards along the route.

FLY, BABY, FLY

As your baby works toward gaining depth perception, he'll want to see more of his environment. Hold him up high to give him a bird's-eye view of his world, and sing for your baby while he flies through the air.

Materials:
- Your strong, safe hands
- Interesting things to look at, inside or outside the house

Learning Skills:	• Balance
	• Head and body control
	• Visual tracking and depth perception

What to Do:

1. Hold your baby tucked under your arm like a football or across your hands like a platter.

2. Lift him up and down, swirl him around, and let him see the world from these new heights. Sing one of the following songs as you soar your baby through the air.

   Go in and out the Window
   Go in and out the window,
   Go in and out the window,
   Go in and out the window,
   As we have done before.

   Pop Goes the Weasel
   All around the mulberry bush,
   The monkey chased the weasel.
   The monkey thought 'twas all in fun,
   Pop! Goes the weasel!

Variation: Sing any song that lends itself to body movement, such as "On Top of Spaghetti," "Row Your Boat," "Sailing-Sailing," or "Wheels on the Bus." If you like, create your own songs to fit the activity.

Safety: Hold your baby securely so he won't be afraid and so you won't drop him during the flying fun.

GONE FiSHiN'

Children of all ages love fishing games, so why not start them young? Your baby will enjoy the element of surprise as she uses her problem-solving skills to get what she wants.

Materials:
- 1 yard of rope
- Colorful toy
- Masking tape
- Table

Learning Skills:	• Anticipation of events • Cause and effect • Object permanence • Problem solving

What to Do:

1. Tie one end of the rope around a colorful toy.

2. Set the rope on a table, with the toy hanging off the table, out of sight.

3. Secure the other end of the rope to the table with a piece of masking tape.

4. Set your baby on your lap, facing the table and rope.

5. Remove the tape and let your baby hold the end of the rope.

6. Give her time to experiment with the rope.

7. Encourage her to pull the rope toward her, saying words like, "What's that?" or, "Where's the toy?" As your baby pulls the rope, the toy will appear at the other end of the table, for a delightful surprise.

8. See if your baby can figure out how to get the toy to her hands.

Variation: Instead of hiding the toy, place it in plain view so your baby can try to figure out how to get it using the rope.

Safety: Watch your baby at all times, so she doesn't become entangled in the rope.

HATS OFF

Your baby is just getting used to recognizing faces, when you introduce the Hats Off game! Your baby won't be fooled for long, but he'll enjoy the fun of taking off the hat and putting it back on again.

Materials:
- Variety of hats
- Infant seat
- Your face and head

Learning Skills:	• Cause and effect • Coping with stranger anxiety • Object constancy (an object remains the same even if altered) • Social interaction

What to Do:

1. Collect a variety of hats around the house, or buy inexpensive hats from a thrift shop or party store. Try to include a baseball cap, a knit cap, a funny hat, a firefighter's hat, a clown hat, a bowler, a beret, a bathing cap, or a fancy, feathery hat. (Don't include masks in your play. They tend to scare babies at this young age.)

2. Place your baby in his infant seat on the floor and sit facing him.

3. Put the first hat on your head and make a funny face as you say something interesting, such as, "Look at me!" or, "I'm a firefighter!"

4. Lean toward your baby so he can grasp the hat and pull it off, or pull the hat off yourself.

5. Repeat several times with one hat before moving on to another hat.

Variation: Place a hat on your baby, as well as on yourself, and look at yourselves in the mirror.

Safety: Sometimes babies get scared when people's appearances change. If your baby starts to get upset, put the hat on only briefly, then remove it and show him you're still Mom/Dad. If he continues to be upset, play the game at a later date.

KiCKER

Here's a game that's a challenge to both you and your baby, and it's great exercise for her as she bicycles her little legs around and around. This is a great game for building muscle strength and coordination, and it is also just plain fun for both of you!

Materials:
- Large plastic beach ball or other plastic ball, 2 to 3 feet in diameter
- Soft blanket on a soft surface

Learning Skills:	• Cause and effect • Coordination • Gross motor development

What to Do:

1. Lay your baby on a soft blanket, on her back.

2. Guide your baby's legs up in the air.

3. Place a ball on your baby's feet and try to keep the ball in the air while your baby kicks her legs.

4. Turn the ball as your baby kicks her feet, and see if you can keep the ball up as it spins!

Variation: Drop the ball on your baby's legs from a short distance and see if she kicks at the ball. If she succeeds, praise her. Otherwise, keep trying until she makes a kick or loses interest.

Safety: Be sure your baby is on a soft surface, as her kicking can overexcite her and cause her to bang herself against the floor. Watch that the ball doesn't hit your baby in the face, for an unwelcome surprise.

LITTLE ENGINE

Now that your baby can sit up with support, play a game of Little Engine and take him on a little trip. He'll enjoy the ride, the view, and the fun with you along the way. All you need is a simple cardboard box!

Materials:
- Cardboard box, approximately 2-by-1½-feet wide, and 1-foot tall
- Soft blankets or towels
- Length of rope, approximately 6 feet long

Learning Skills:	• Balance • Head and neck control • Visual tracking

What to Do:

1. Find a box that will hold your baby while he sits up, and cut down the height of the box so your baby is supported, but can see over the top.

2. Punch two holes in the front end of the box on either side, about halfway down.

3. Insert rope ends into the holes and knot the ends securely.

4. Line the box with blankets or towels, to give your baby comfort and support.

5. Grasp the loop of the rope and gently pull your baby around the house or yard in his Little Engine.

Variation: Paint the box to look like a small train engine for added fun. Or paint it to look like a plane, car, boat, or other favorite vehicle.

Safety: Be sure to pull your baby slowly so he doesn't get a neck injury and isn't startled by sudden moves. Be careful to avoid steps and other uneven surfaces.

MOVERS AND SHAKERS

Turn your baby's arm and leg movements into a symphony of noise. She'll soon learn to make deliberate movements to create the response.

Materials:

- Elastic hair "scrunchies" or other small fabric-covered elastic bands, 1 or 2 inches in diameter
- Needle and thread
- Bells, small rattles, or other noise-makers
- Soft blanket or infant seat

Learning Skills:	• Auditory locating • Cause and effect • Motor control (for left and right sides of the body)

What to Do:

1. Sew bells, small rattles, or other small noisemakers to the outside of the hair bands.

2. Lay your baby on her back on a soft blanket or in an infant seat.

3. Slip the bands onto your baby's wrists and ankles.

4. Watch your baby reflexively shake her arms and kick her legs, which will cause sounds. Then watch as she learns how to make the sounds, as she moves her arms and legs deliberately.

Variation: Sew the noisemakers onto small socks or mittens, and place them on your baby's hands and feet.

Safety: Make sure the noisemakers are securely sewn to the bands, so they can't come off and be swallowed by your baby. Don't sew on any objects that are hard or have pointed ends or sharp edges.

OLD MACDONALD

Your baby is now ready for advanced puppet play! Use your imagination to create a whole series of puppet people based on your favorite children's books. We've chosen "Old MacDonald" for this one.

Materials:
- Garden glove
- 5 colorful 1-inch pom-poms: beige, pink, black, yellow, white
- Glue gun
- 10 small, wiggly eyes
- Colorful felt scraps

Learning Skills:	• Language development • Social interaction • Visual tracking

What to Do:

1. Buy five pom-poms—skin-colored (beige) for the farmer, pink for the pig, black for the cow, yellow for the chick, and white for the goat.

2. Glue the pom-poms to the tops of the garden glove fingers (on the palm side).

3. Add wiggly eyes. Use felt scraps to create a pink snout for the pig, large horns for the cow, yellow feathers for the chick, and tiny horns for the goat.

4. Allow glue to dry thoroughly.

5. Place your baby in your lap or in an infant seat, facing you.

6. Slip the glove onto your hand and sing "Old MacDonald Had a Farm," wiggling each finger puppet as you mention it.

Variation: Instead of "Old MacDonald," make "The Three Little Pigs," with three pink pom-poms for the pigs, one black pom-pom for the wolf, and one white pom-pom for the wolf in sheep's clothing.

Safety: Be sure the pom-poms and other accessories are securely glued to the glove. Don't let your baby put the glove in his mouth.

OPEN AND CLOSE

For several months after your baby is born, she has a reflex to grasp objects in her palm, but she has trouble letting go. Here's a game to help her gain further control of her hands and her grasp reflex.

Materials:
- Small toys easily grasped in your baby's hands, such as rattles, stuffed animals, teething rings, blocks, and so on
- Table or highchair

Learning Skills:	• Grasping and releasing • Fine motor development • Fine muscle control

What to Do:

1. Collect a variety of small toys that easily fit in your baby's hands.

2. Seat your baby in your lap next to the table or in her highchair.

3. Place a small toy near your baby, so she has to reach a little to grasp it.

4. Encourage her to take the toy.

5. After she has grasped the toy and enjoyed it for a moment, gently peel open her fingers and remove the toy.

6. Place it back on the table.

7. While your baby's hands are free, sing the following song as you open, shut, then clap your baby's hands.

Open, Close Them
Open, close them, open, close them,
Give a little clap!
Open, close them, open close them,
Put them in your lap!

Variation: Instead of unpeeling your baby's fingers, offer her another toy. As your baby reaches and grasps for the second toy, she should release the first toy. If she accidentally drops a toy from her hand, say, "Whoops! You dropped it!" and pick up the toy. See if she will repeat the drop.

Safety: Since your baby is sure to put all toys into her mouth during these months, be sure they are clean and have no sharp edges.

PLAY PUPPET

As your baby's vision improves, he can see objects more clearly at greater distances. To work on his focusing and tracking skills, keep a Play Puppet "handy" for feeding, changing, or play time.

Materials:
- Clean white sock
- Permanent felt-tip markers

Learning Skills:	• Language development • Social interaction • Visual acuity

What to Do:

1. Buy a pair of white socks, large enough to fit over your hands.

2. Use permanent felt-tip markers to draw eyes, eyebrows, noses, and ears on the socks' toes. Outline the heels to create mouths, and draw red tongues inside the folds.

3. Place your baby in your lap, on the changing table, or in his infant seat.

4. Slip one puppet onto your hand and entertain your baby with songs, rhymes, or simple conversation. Slip the second puppet onto your other hand for two-handed fun.

Variation: Decorate baby socks to make a set of baby Play Puppets, then slip the baby puppets onto your baby's little hands while you do your puppet act. If you prefer, create three-dimensional puppets by sewing wiggly eyes, pom-pom noses, felt lips and tongues, and yarn hair onto the socks.

Safety: If you sew on the facial features, make sure they are securely attached, and don't let your baby put the socks in his mouth. If you create the puppets with markers, don't let your baby suck on the sock, since the ink might come off.

PONY RiDES

As your baby increases her neck strength and head control, you can take her on some gentle pony rides. Choose a favorite nursery rhyme, or sing the ones below.

Materials:
- Your knee
- Small, soft blanket or towel

Learning Skills:	• Balance
	• Head and neck control
	• Language development
	• Social interaction

What to Do:

1. Lay a small, soft blanket or towel over your knee, for your baby's comfort.

2. Seat your baby on your knee, facing you, and hold her arms for support.

3. As you recite a rhyme, gently bounce your baby up and down.

4. Repeat the rhyme several times before moving on to another. Following are some rhymes to try:

Humpty Dumpty
Humpty Dumpty sat on a wall,
Humpty Dumpty had a great fall.
All the king's horses and all the king's men,
Couldn't put Humpty together again.

To Market, to Market
To market, to market, to buy a fat pig,
Home again, home again, jiggety-jig.
To market, to market, to buy a fat hog,
Home again, home again, jiggety-jog.

One, Two, Bounce My Shoe
One, two, bounce my shoe;
Three, four, tap the floor;
Five, six, give a kick;
Seven, eight, legs stand straight;
Nine, ten, start again.

Variation: Face your baby away from you and play the game again.

Safety: Don't bounce your baby too hard, and always hold her so she doesn't fall.

RAIN BATH

Help your baby learn about his environment by expanding his world through his senses. Water play provides the perfect sensory-motor stimulation, so turn bath time into a sensory experience!

Materials:
- Turkey skewer
- Plastic bottle, such as a liquid dish-washing bottle or ketchup/mustard bottle
- Baby bathtub or regular bathtub

Learning Skills:	• Enjoyment of the environment • Sensory-motor development • Social interaction

What to Do:

1. Use a turkey skewer to poke holes on the bottom and sides of the plastic bottle, making holes about one inch apart.

2. Place your baby in a baby bathtub or get into a regular bathtub with him, if you like. Lower your baby into the water gently, to give him time to get comfortable with the strange sensation.

3. Fill the plastic bottle with bathtub water.

4. Hold the bottle up so your baby can see the water pour out from the holes.

5. Hold the bottle over your baby's body and let the water gently tickle him.

6. If your baby's game, hold the bottle over his head to make it rain!

Variation: Use plastic bottles for other water play. A plastic ketchup bottle makes a nice squirter, as does a turkey baster. A spray bottle for misting plants is great for a gentle water experience.

Safety: Try not to get water in your baby's eyes, especially if the water is soapy. If your baby doesn't like getting his face wet, just trickle the water on his body.

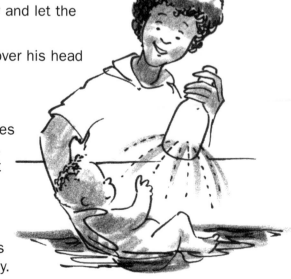

RiDE A HORSEY

Take your baby for a horsey ride—without leaving home! Your body provides the transportation, and your voice creates the necessary sounds. So saddle up your baby and trot her around the corral.

Materials:
- Comfortable chair
- Your leg
- Small towel

Learning Skills:	• Balance
	• Head control
	• Motor control
	• Social interaction

What to Do:

1. Remove your shoes and sit in a comfortable chair, with your legs crossed.

2. Place a small towel on your ankle.

3. Sit your baby on the towel, facing you, with her arms outstretched in front of her.

4. Hold your baby's hands and gently move your leg up and down, to give your baby a horsey ride. As your baby rides, sing one of the following songs:

Ride a Cock-Horse
Ride a cock-horse to Banbury Cross,
To see a fine lady upon a white horse;
With rings on her fingers and bells on her toes,
She shall have music wherever she goes.

London Bridge
London Bridge is falling down,
Falling down, falling down,
London Bridge is falling down,
My fair lady.

Variation: Place your baby on your knee instead of your ankle, and move your leg up and down for the horsey ride. Face your baby away from you, for a different perspective.

Safety: DO NOT bounce your baby too hard.
Keep the movement slow and gentle to avoid hurting your baby's delicate neck.

ROAMING SPOTLIGHT

To help your baby enhance his visual skills, play a game of Roaming Spotlight. This is a quiet game you can play at night, just before your baby goes to sleep, or to calm him down.

Materials:
- Dark room
- Flashlight

Learning Skills:	• Cause and effect • Depth perception • Understanding of environment • Visual tracking

What to Do:

1. Find a room that can be made completely dark.

2. Sit on a chair or on the floor, with your baby in your lap.

3. With the lights off, turn on the flashlight and shine it on the wall, catching your baby's attention.

4. Say something about the light, such as, "Oh, look at the light!"

5. Move the light beam around slowly, resting it on interesting objects.

6. Say something about the object as it lights up, such as, "There's baby's teddy bear!"

7. Continue moving the light around until your baby grows tired of the game.

Variation: Let your baby hold the flashlight, with your support, and see if he can figure out how to manipulate the light. Or give him a small flashlight of his own.

Safety: Don't shine the light in your baby's eyes. If your baby becomes afraid in the dark, turn on a night-light, which should not diminish the flashlight's beam too much.

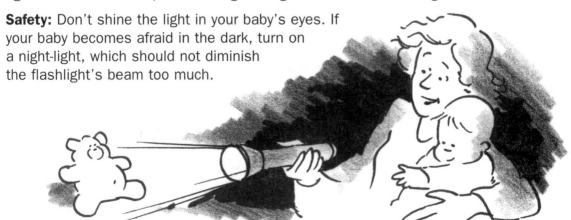

SPEEDY SPiDER

This tickle-me game gets more and more exciting every time you play. It also helps your baby get better acquainted with her body, and teaches her to enjoy social play.

Materials:
- Your lap or infant seat
- Your fingers

Learning Skills:	• Anticipation • Body awareness • Sensory stimulation • Social interaction

What to Do:

1. Remove your baby's clothes (diaper optional).

2. Place your baby on your lap or in her infant seat.

3. Recite the following rhyme and do the correspond finger movements.

Itsy-Bitsy Spider
The itsy-bitsy spider went up the waterspout,
(walk your fingers up your baby's chest to her chin)
Down came the rain and washed the spider out,
(wiggle your fingers down her chest, like falling rain)
Out came the sun and dried up all the rain,
(pat your baby's tummy, to "dry" her off)
And the itsy-bitsy spider went up the spout again.
(walk your fingers up your baby's chest again)

4. Repeat the game, moving faster and faster each time you play.

Variation: Instead of using your fingers, use a small soft toy, preferably a spider. If you use some other toy animal, change "spider" in the song to the name of the animal.

Safety: Don't tickle your baby too much, or it will irritate, instead of delight, her.

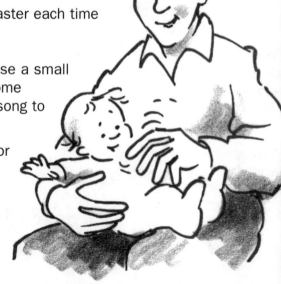

SQUISH IT

At this age, your baby will try to pick up small objects with his fat little fingers. Play a game of Squish It to help your baby gain independence and practice his fine motor skills. As a bonus, your baby might even get some good nutrition!

Materials:
- Bib
- Floor covering (optional)
- Highchair with a seat belt
- Ripe banana

Learning Skills:	• Autonomy/independence • Fine motor development • Self-help skills—eating

What to Do:
1. Cover your baby's clothes with a bib.

2. If you want, lay a floor covering on the kitchen floor and place a high-chair on top of the covering.

3. Place your baby in the highchair and secure him with a seat belt.

4. Divide a ripe banana into chunks and place the pieces on the highchair tray.

5. Let your baby explore the properties of the banana—with his hands, face, and mouth.

Variation: Try a variety of soft foods, such as a ripe peach (without the pit), a plate of Jell-O, or a small bowl of cooked, cooled rice, oatmeal, or mashed potatoes.

Safety: Always remain with your baby while he eats, to ensure he doesn't choke.

UPSY-DAiSY

Your baby will soon lose two reflexes she had at birth—the grasp reflex and the baby-doll reflex (she opens her eyes when she sits up)—as she gains more control over her movements. While she still has them, play Upsy-Daisy to take advantage of these reflexes!

Materials:
• Soft, unslippery surface
• Your hands

Learning Skills:	• Anticipation and surprise
	• Grasping
	• Head and neck control
	• Social interaction

What to Do:

1. Lay your baby on a soft, unslippery surface, such as a carpet.

2. Sit at her feet, facing her.

3. Place your thumbs in your baby's palms and let her grasp them. As she does, wrap your fingers around the backs of her hands.

4. Slowly pull your baby to a sitting position and say, "Upsy-Daisy" as you go.

5. After your baby's had a moment to see your happy face and enjoy the game, lay her back down and play again.

Variation: Place your baby in a supported sitting position, then let her grasp your thumbs and raise her to a standing position. This is great exercise for her legs.

Safety: Be sure to hold on to your baby's hands in case she lets go of her grasp. Move slowly so your baby doesn't get a neck injury.

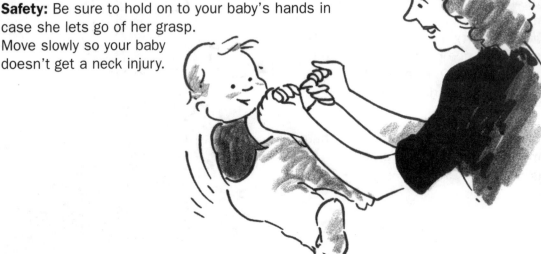

WATER WiGGLER

As your baby grows and develops, his five senses contribute to his knowledge of himself and the world around him. Playing in a tub of water provides a complete sensory experience, along with a lot of fun!

Materials:
- Bathtub
- Your hands

Learning Skills:	• Motor control • Sensory exploration • Social interaction • Understanding of environment

What to Do:

1. Run a warm bathtub of water for your baby (and yourself, if you like).

2. Slowly place your baby in the water, allowing him to get used to the water.

3. Show your baby the properties of the water by lightly drizzling, splashing, and pouring water over him.

4. When your baby is ready to play Water Wiggle, hold him firmly on his tummy with both hands, and move him slowly back and forth over the surface of the water, being sure his head is above the surface.

5. Make motorboat sounds while you wiggle your baby back and forth in the water. Let your baby rest a few minutes between rides.

Variation: Place your baby on his back and repeat the ride. Or place some toys in the water and move your baby toward them, then pull him away when he makes contact with the toys.

Safety: Be sure your baby's head does not get submerged and the water does not get on his face, in his eyes, or in his mouth. Make sure the water is not too cold or too hot.

SiX MONTHS TO NiNE MONTHS

Your baby becomes a whirlwind of activity as she learns to manipulate her body from head to foot and from chest to fingers and toes. She'll soon be sitting, creeping, crawling, even standing, as she practices her gross motor movement. At the same time, she'll change her grasp from palmer (the whole hand) to pincer (finger and thumb).

Your baby still loves to put things in her mouth, but she's better at using her hands for holding, dropping, and throwing. And she's even getting better at putting the right things in her mouth—food. As you introduce your baby to solids, give her a chance to hold her own spoon and cup, so she can begin the basics of self-help skills. The results are sure to be messy at first, but soon she'll be able to feed herself without needing a hose for cleaning up!

Your baby is taking in your words and trying to make further sense of them. She understands the words she hears frequently, such as "No!" and "Want a bottle?" and she understand the words she cares about, such as "Daddy," "Mommy," and "Doggy." She can "talk" using body language, by pointing, reaching, waving bye-bye. And she is better able to control her facial expressions to make her needs known.

Your baby begins to have a stronger sense of self, too, as she separates from mom and dad and crawls away on her own. This is a scary time for her—a kind of push-pull toward and away from parents—but she's ready to explore her environment on her own, under your supervision.

Your baby also likes to play with you, as well as other babies her own age, so supply her with lots of opportunities for social interaction. She may have a little stranger anxiety or fear of parent separation; help her work through it by playing games that teach social development and object permanence.

It's never too soon to enhance your baby's self-esteem, either. While you're playing some of the games in this section, set your baby up for success, and watch her gain the confidence to tackle new challenges. If she feels good about herself and her abilities, there will be no stopping her!

So get on your hands and knees and try to keep up with your busy baby!

ABRACADABRA

Play a magical game of "Where did it go?" with your baby, and make a toy disappear right before his eyes—without mirrors! He will soon be on to you, and will realize that the toy didn't disappear, but is still in your hand.

Materials:
• Small toy

Learning Skills:	• Cognitive skills • Eye/hand coordination • Object permanence

What to Do:

1. Find a bright toy small enough to fit into your hand.

2. Lay your baby on his back and let him see the toy.

3. Let your baby hold the toy for a few minutes to explore it.

4. Gently take the toy from his hands and place it in your palm.

5. Close both hands and show your baby your closed fists.

6. Ask your baby, "Where did it go?"

7. When your baby looks puzzled, open your hand and show him the toy, saying, "Here it is!"

8. Repeat the game, alternating hands and toys.

Variation: Paint your nails with colorful nail polish, or draw little faces on your nails with felt-tip pens. Show your baby your fingers, wiggle

them, then fold them into your palms, one at a time, to make them disappear. Bring them back one at a time, then hide them again.

Safety: Be sure the toy is not too small, so your baby won't choke on it when he examines it.

AT THE ZOO

As your baby begins to talk, she loves making sounds. So take an imaginary trip to the zoo and learn about animals while you increase your baby's listening and language skills.

Materials:
- Stuffed animals or large pictures of animals
- Infant seat
- Your voice

Learning Skills:	• Auditory recognition • Classification skills • Language development • Social interaction

What to Do:
1. Collect a variety of stuffed animals or large pictures of animals.
2. Seat your baby in her infant seat and sit facing her.
3. Hold up an animal or picture next to your face, so your baby can see your mouth, then make the animal's sound.
4. Give your baby a chance to imitate the sound, then repeat the sound.
5. Hold up the next animal or picture and make the appropriate sound.
6. Repeat for all the animals or pictures.
7. Hold up the animals or pictures again, this time pausing a moment before making the animal sounds, so your baby can anticipate them.

Variation: Some babies learn better visually, while others learn by auditory stimulation. If your baby has an auditory preference, try making the sound first, then holding up the animal or picture.

Safety: Don't make the sounds too loud; you don't want to scare your baby.

"MEOW..."

BEANIE BABIES

Make your own Beanie Babies for all kinds of fun. Sew a small animal shape, fill it with beans, and let your baby explore its properties. Then try the games below with your Beanie Baby.

Materials:
- 2 terry cloth washcloths or similar fabric
- 2 cups of beans
- Needle and thread
- Permanent felt-tip pens

Learning Skills:	• Cognitive/thinking skills
	• Emotional development
	• Fine motor development
	• Imaginative play

What to Do:

1. Cut out two identical animal shapes from the washcloths; keep the shapes simple. A bear, mouse, or frog are all fun and simple shapes.

2. Sew the shapes together, leaving the head area open.

3. Turn the animal pouch right-side out, so the seams are inside, and fill the animal with beans to about three-quarter full.

4. Stitch the opening closed.

5. Draw a face and other details with permanent felt-tip pens.

6. Give the Beanie Baby to your baby to explore for a few minutes.

7. Show your baby how to play with his new toy: drop it, throw it, stack it, lay it on body parts, hide it, make it move and talk, kiss it, hold it, and fold it.

Variation: Make a larger Beanie Baby using hand towels. Make a whole bunch of Beanie Babies for your baby to enjoy.

Safety: Be sure the Beanie Baby is securely sewn together, so no beans fall out. Buy small beans that won't choke your baby if he gets ahold of some.

DRUM BEAT

Even at this young age, your baby has rhythm! She loves to pound and make noise, so use those skills to turn her into an amateur percussionist. Here are several ways to enjoy the beat of the drums.

Materials:
- Highchair and tray
- Wooden spoon, basting brush, and other "drumsticks"
- Foil, metal pot, plastic bowl, pie pan, newspaper, and other items to pound

Learning Skills:	• Cause and effect • Listening skills • Rhythm and coordination

What to Do:

1. Seat your baby in the highchair with the tray attached.

2. Offer her a wooden spoon and show her how to pound it on the tray.

3. Next offer her the basting brush and any other "drumsticks," one at a time.

4. Then offer her different items to beat, such as a sheet of foil, a metal pot, a plastic bowl, a pie pan, a newspaper, and so on.

5. Stuff cotton in your ears so you won't get a headache! (Just kidding!)

Variation: Seat your baby on the floor, set out all the items at once, and let her go to town on her drumming equipment. Make her a drum by covering the open end of an oatmeal box with wax paper, and let her tap it with a small wooden spoon.

Safety: Watch that your baby doesn't hit herself or others with the drumsticks.

49

GOTCHA!

The "I'm gonna getcha" game gets exciting when your baby turns half a year old. He's now aware of his environment, he knows his parents well, and he's used to a little surprise now and then. Go get 'em!

Materials:
- Soft blanket
- Your wiggling fingers

Learning Skills:	• Anticipation and surprise • Expression of feelings • Motor control • Social interaction

What to Do:

1. Spread a soft blanket on the floor and place your baby on the blanket, on his tummy.

2. Move across the room and get down on your hands and knees.

3. Call to your baby, "I'm gonna getcha!" as you begin crawling toward him, wiggling your fingers and alternating your hands.

4. Repeat the chant as you get closer and closer, smiling and giggling as you speak to show your baby you're just having fun.

5. When you reach your baby, place your wiggling hands on your baby's back and give him a quick tickle, as you say, "Gotcha!"

6. Repeat until your baby grows tired of the game.

Variation: Come up behind your baby, instead of in front of him, for a surprising change. If your baby tries to escape by creeping away, move slowly to give him a chance.

Safety: Have another parent "protect" your baby as you approach him, to relieve his fears if he seems upset.

HAPPY!

Your baby now has a wide range of emotions—from joy, to sadness, to anger, even to guilt and pride. Here's a game to help her express positive emotions, while learning her body parts.

Materials:
- Infant seat
- Your body parts
- Your voice

Learning Skills:	• Coordination and mimicry • Emotional expression • Gross and fine motor development • Language development

What to Do:

1. Seat your baby in her infant seat on the floor.

2. Sing the song, "If You're Happy and You Know It," and move the appropriate body part for your baby as you sing.

If You're Happy and You Know It
If you're happy and you know it, clap your hands.
If you're happy and you know it, clap your hands.
If you're happy and you know it,
Then your hands will really show it.
If you're happy and you know it, clap your hands.

3. Repeat the song, replacing "clap your hands" with "stomp your feet," "nod your head," "wave your arms," "bend your knees," "bounce your butt," and "blow a kiss."

Variation: Make up your own lyrics, adding other body parts, such as fingers, toes, tongue, hair, or even your baby's toys.

Safety: Move your baby's body gently, so you don't hurt her while you play this active game.

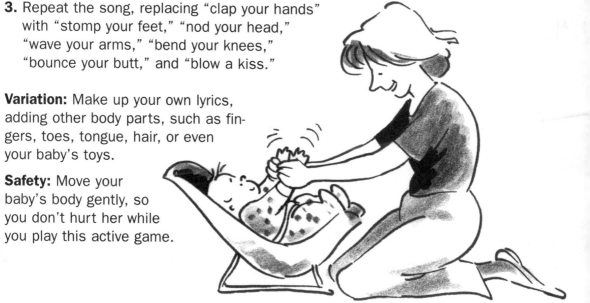

iCE PALACE

This is a fun activity to play with your baby in the bathtub. It will keep him occupied and entertained while he learns about the properties of water.

Materials:
- Ice tray or molds
- Baby bathtub
- Balloons
- Milk carton
- Food coloring
- Small plastic or sink-and-float items

Learning Skills:	• Cause and effect • Fine motor development • Object permanence • Scientific properties

What to Do:

1. Fill ice trays or molds, balloons, milk cartons, and other containers with water; tint each item a different color with food coloring, and freeze overnight.

2. Fill a baby bathtub with warm water and gently lower your baby into the water.

3. Place the colorful ice cubes into the tub and let your baby try to pick them up, push them underwater, or just watch them bounce.

4. Peel the balloons off the frozen water and place the frozen balloon shapes into the tub. Let your baby explore the properties of the frozen balloons.

5. Peel the milk cartons off the ice blocks and place the frozen blocks into the tub.

6. Set small plastic figures or other sink-and-float items on top of the ice blocks. Let your baby watch the figures drop off the blocks as they melt.

Variation: Insert small plastic toys inside ice cubes before freezing. As the ice melts, watch the toys appear. Freeze the water in layers of different colors, then watch the layers disappear as the ice melts.

Safety: Do not leave baby unattended in the tub. Have all materials ready to use before play. Make sure the plastic figures and sink-and-float items are not too small, so your baby won't choke on them.

PICK A PEA

Isn't it amazing how those little fingers are able to pick out the tiniest particles from your carpet, when only a short time ago, they were just an extra appendage? Give those busy fingers something to pick up with a game of Pick a Pea.

Materials:
- Highchair and tray
- ½ cup frozen peas, still frozen

Learning Skills:	• Eye/hand coordination • Fine motor development • Introduction to new flavors • Self-help—eating

What to Do:

1. Seat your baby in the highchair with an attached tray.

2. Pour a half cup of frozen peas onto the tray.

3. Let your baby enjoy the challenge of picking up the peas and putting them in her mouth.

4. If she needs help getting started, demonstrate the process a few times.

Variation: Substitute frozen fruit pieces for peas, if you prefer, but be sure the bites are small enough that your baby won't choke on them.

Safety: Watch your baby during play. She may choke if she tries to stuff too many peas in her mouth at once.

POP GOES THE PARENT

Babies enjoy the game of jack-in-the-box, but the game becomes even more fun when the parent becomes Jack! All you have to do is find a great big box, and you'll delight your baby with a great big surprise.

Materials:
- Large box
- Yourself

Learning Skills:	• Anticipation and surprise
	• Emotional expression
	• Object permanence
	• Social interaction

What to Do:

1. Get a box large enough for you to fit inside. Set it in the living room and get inside.

2. Have the other parent bring your baby into the room, asking, "Where's Mommy/Daddy?" and singing the jack-in-the-box song:

Jack-in-the-Box
Jack-in-the-box, you've gone away,
Won't you come out and play?
Jack-in-the-box, you're hidden away,
Pop out so we can play!

3. Have the parent in the box pop out after the last line of the song.

4. Switch parents and repeat the game.

Variation: If you only have a small box, cut an opening in the bottom and slip your hand into the box through the hole. Place a puppet on your hand, then close the box top. Sing the song, then pop the puppet out of the box at the end.

Safety: Pop out slowly and quietly so you don't scare your baby. The idea here is to surprise and delight your baby, not terrify him!

PORCUPINE PAL

Create a plaything that can be used three ways—as a puppet, as a texture toy, and as a fine motor manipulator. The Porcupine Pal does all three, so plan on spending lots of time with your baby and this fun toy.

Materials:
- Garden glove
- Fake fur
- Needle and thread
- Fabric scraps

Learning Skills:	• Fine motor development • Language development • Sensory exploration • Social skills

What to Do:

1. Sew fake fur on the back of the garden glove, creating the porcupine's "quills."

2. Sew fabric pieces all over the glove, to create a variety of textures.

3. Add eyes, nose, mouth, and other details with bits of fabric.

4. Slip the glove onto your hand to make Porcupine Pal come alive. Sing, talk, and move the puppet around your baby.

5. Let your baby have a turn wearing the glove puppet, too.

Variation: Instead of a porcupine, make your baby's favorite animal using fabric pieces, felt-tip pens, and a little imagination. Use both gloves if you want a girl and a boy, a mom and a dad, or two animals.

Safety: Be sure the fabric pieces are securely attached so your baby doesn't choke on loose scraps.

SiLLY SPOT

Body awareness becomes an important developmental task as your baby learns to sit, creep, crawl, and eventually walk. This fun body discovery game will help your baby find the Silly Spot!

Materials:
- Infant seat or the floor
- Small colorful stickers

Learning Skills:	• Body awareness • Object permanence • Problem solving • Social interaction • Visual scanning

What to Do:

1. Dress your baby only in a diaper.

2. Prop your baby up in an infant seat or on the floor if he's learned to sit.

3. Sit opposite him and have a batch of small colorful stickers nearby.

4. Show your baby one of the stickers, then quickly stick it somewhere on his body, without showing him where it's going. You can do this by hiding the sticker between two fingers, then placing your hand on a body part.

5. Remove your hand and ask your baby, "Where's the sticker?"

6. Begin to look on your baby's body for the sticker. Check his hands, then say, "Noooo, not there." Check his arms, then say, "Noooo, not there." Keep checking until you discover the sticker, then say, "Here it is!" and show your baby the sticker on his body.

7. Repeat, placing the sticker in different places each time.

8. After a few times, give your baby a chance to search for the sticker himself. Give him hints if he needs them.

Variation: Place stickers on your body and let your baby search for them, with your help.

Safety: Since the stickers are small and can be swallowed, be sure to keep them out of your baby's mouth.

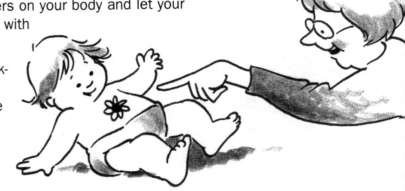

SINK OR FLOAT

As your baby begins to understand how the world works, you can help her begin to classify items according to similar properties. At this age she'll think these differences and similarities are magical, but soon she'll learn they can all be explained scientifically.

Materials:

- 5 items that sink, such as stones, cans, spoons, bells, a key chain, and so on
- 5 items that float, such as soap, plastic toys, pencils, hairbrush, sponges, and so on
- Baby bathtub

Learning Skills:	• Beginning scientific properties • Classification skills

What to Do:

1. Fill a baby bathtub with warm water and gently lower your baby into the water.

2. Place one floating item into the tub and say, "It floats!"

3. After a minute, place a sinkable item into the tub and say, "It sinks!"

4. Alternate items to keep your baby's interest, then let her drop the items in the tub herself.

Variation: Put all the floating items in the tub, one at a time, and watch them float. Then drop in an item that sinks and watch baby's surprise as it falls to the bottom. Repeat, telling your baby what is happening.

Safety: Never leave your baby alone in or near water.

SNOW SCAPE

As your baby learns about the many different textures in his environment, you can add to his world by providing some new experiences. Use real snow for this game, or make your own using a blender.

Materials:
- Clean snow
- Highchair and tray
- Towel
- Food color (optional)

Learning Skills:	• Cognitive skills
	• Fine motor development
	• Properties of snow—touch, texture, temperature

What to Do:

1. Collect some clean snow from the yard, or make your own by whirling ice cubes in a blender until they are soft and flaky.

2. Seat your baby in the highchair and securely attach the tray.

3. Place a cup of snow onto the tray.

4. Let your baby explore the properties of the snow with his hands and mouth.

5. If your baby is reluctant to touch the snow, demonstrate how to play with this strange, cold substance.

6. As the snow melts on the tray, wipe it off with a towel and add another cup of still-frozen snow.

Variation: For added visual stimulation, tint the snow with a few drops of food coloring. Provide your baby with some toys to make the play more interesting; try a cup or other scooper, a plastic doll, a small ball, and so on.

Safety: If using real snow, be sure it is clean, because your baby will put it in his mouth.

SQUEEZERS

Your baby gains gross motor strength during this time, but she also works on her fine motor skills as her tiny fingers explore the world of temperature, texture, and touch.

Materials:

- Variety of squeezable objects, such as Play-Doh, clay, marshmallows, sponges, squeeze toys, stress balls, Koosh balls
- Highchair

Learning Skills:	• Classification skills • Cognitive development • Exploration of the senses—touch • Fine motor development

What to Do:

1. Collect a variety of squeezable items, including a few that make noise.

2. Seat your baby in her highchair and securely attach the tray.

3. Place one squeezable item on the tray and let your baby explore it. Encourage her to squeeze it and to feel the texture, resistance, temperature, and so on.

4. After a few minutes, replace the first item with another squeezable item.

5. Repeat until your baby has explored all the squeezable items.

Variation: Place the items in small thin socks, so your baby can't see them. Set all the items on the tray and let your baby explore their similarities and differences through the socks.

Safety: Supervise your baby at all times to be sure she doesn't eat the items.

TIPSY TEETER-TOTTER

Balance is a tricky task for your baby to master in those early months. At first he has difficulty just balancing that big head. But soon he'll enjoy being challenged with games like Tipsy Teeter-Totter!

Materials:
- Small towel
- Your leg

Learning Skills:	• Balance
	• Development of trust
	• Social interaction

What to Do:

1. Place a small towel on your thigh as a cushion for your baby.

2. Seat your baby on your thigh, facing you.

3. Hold your baby by his arms, then move your hands down the length of his arms to his fingers, so you're holding on lightly.

4. As you balance your baby on your leg, move your leg around slowly.

5. Try to let go of one hand, then the other, while balancing your baby, being ready to catch him if needed.

6. Turn your baby the other direction and play again.

Variation: Stretch out your leg, prop your foot on a chair, and seat your baby on your lower leg instead of your thigh.

Safety: Be ready to catch and hold your baby steady at all times, in case he loses his balance.

TOUCH 'N' TELL

Your baby's environment offers a lot of stimulation for her five senses. Provide your baby with a rich variety of interesting things to explore, and she'll have a great time with her hands and mouth.

Materials:
- Variety of favorite foods
- Highchair
- Plastic floor covering

Learning Skills:	• Awareness of the environment • Fine motor development • Science experimentation

What to Do:

1. Prepare a number of interesting foods for your baby to touch, taste, and smell —in very small amounts—such as Jell-O, yogurt, peanut butter, banana, Cheerios, oatmeal, spaghetti, and so on.

2. Spread a plastic floor covering in the kitchen, and place the highchair on the covering.

3. Seat your baby in the highchair and place one food item on the tray.

4. Let your baby play with the food for a few minutes, exploring it with her hands and mouth.

5. Remove the food and offer a second item for exploration.

6. Watch your baby's expression as she examines each new food. Make sure to name and describe each item as you place it in front of your baby.

Variation: Present only one food item in a larger quantity, so your baby can finger-paint with it, play with it, pound it, squish it, and enjoy it.

Safety: Be sure to keep an eye on your baby so she doesn't choke on any of the foods.

TUNNEL TRIP

As your baby begins to move around the room, make movement more fun for him with a Tunnel Trip. He'll discover a new way to move himself, and a surprise at the end of the tunnel! All you need is a big box.

Materials:
- Cardboard box, a little larger than your baby's body
- Small baby blanket

Learning Skills:	• Cognitive/thinking skills
	• Depth perception
	• Object permanence
	• Problem solving

What to Do:

1. Find a box a little larger than your baby's body, so he can crawl through easily. Cut both ends off the box to make a tunnel.

2. Place your baby on the floor at one end of the tunnel.

3. Position yourself at the other end of the tunnel and call to your baby. Try to get him to come into the box. If your baby needs help, reach in and gently pull him through the box to the other side.

4. Repeat several times.

5. Place a blanket over your end of the box so your baby can't see you, then reach in and pull your baby through to the other side.

Variation: Sit your baby on the floor, then place the box over him. Peek at him from the top, then remove the box and say, "Peekaboo!"

Safety: Make sure the box isn't too small, and don't leave your baby alone in the box or he might get scared.

UPSTAIRS, DOWNSTAIRS

Crawling seems to be your baby's primary focus during these months. This game helps your baby practice her crawling skills while she learns new ways to get around—as well as up and down!

Materials:
- Stairs
- Interesting toys

Learning Skills:	• Exploration • Gross motor development • Problem solving

What to Do:

1. Find a staircase that is appropriate for your baby to climb. Carpeted staircases are better than those with slippery steps.

2. Sit at the bottom of the stairs with your baby and place a toy on the first step. Let your baby reach up for the toy and retrieve it.

3. Place a toy on the second step and attract your baby's attention to it.

4. As she reaches for it, help her learn to climb the step by bending her knee, and placing her hands on the step.

5. As she grabs the toy, place another toy on the next step for her to retrieve.

Variation: When your baby reaches the top of the stairs, teach her how to get back down. Since babies don't understand the concept of reversibility, you'll have to teach her how to reach out with her foot and ease herself down each step.

Safety: Keep the staircase enclosed with safety gates at the top and the bottom at all times, when not using it for climbing practice.

63

WATCH THE BIRDY

Your baby becomes Super Baby as he flies through the air with the strongest of knees—your knees, that is. Babies love to become airborne, as their parents sail them around on their feet, as high as the birdies fly!

Materials:
- Your clean feet
- Socks

Learning Skills:	• Balance
	• Depth perception
	• Gross motor development
	• Social interaction and trust

What to Do:

1. Put soft socks on your feet to make them comfortable for your baby.

2. Lie down on your back next to your baby.

3. Lift your baby up and onto the soles of your feet, his head facing you and his feet extended away, while you hold his arms.

4. When baby is comfortable and secure, move your legs back and forth to "fly" your baby.

5. Use your imagination as you move your feet to give your baby a variety of flying experiences.

Variation: Lay your baby on your legs instead of your feet, if you prefer, to give him a stronger foundation. Turn him away from you instead of toward you, for a different perspective.

Safety: Be sure to hold your baby securely and make sure he is well-balanced on your feet. Move slowly, not suddenly, so he'll feel safe as he flies.

WHERE DID IT GO?

Soon you won't be able to fool your baby with this game, so you'd better play it now and enjoy it. As the toy disappears, watch your baby try to figure out where it went, and what's going to happen next.

Materials:
- Cardboard paper towel or gift wrap tube
- Permanent felt-tip markers, stickers, and other decorative items (optional)
- Small ball, car, or toy that easily fits inside the tube
- Infant seat

Learning Skills:	• Anticipation and surprise • Cause and effect • Object permanence • Problem solving

What to Do:
1. If you like, decorate a cardboard paper towel or gift wrap tube with permanent felt-tip markers, stickers, and other decorative items to make it more interesting.

2. Place the tube and a small item (ball, car, or toy) on the floor.

3. Seat your baby in her infant seat, on the floor, and sit next to her.

4. Position the tube at a forty-five-degree angle, so one end rests in your baby's lap, and the other end sticks up in the air.

5. Show your baby the small ball or toy and have her watch as you drop it into the top of the tube. Say, "Where did it go?" as you let go of the toy.

6. When the toy lands in your baby's lap, say, "There it is!" and show your baby the newly arrived toy.

7. Repeat the game until your baby grows tired of it.

Variation: Use a number of toys at one time, or use a variety of toys to add to the fun. Have your baby drop the toy in the top and let it land in your lap.

Safety: Make sure the toy isn't small enough to be swallowed by your baby.

NiNE MONTHS TO TWELVE MONTHS

There's no stopping your baby now! He's moving fast and he's on his way to cruising (holding onto furniture as he walks), walking, running, and beyond. As your baby's skills grow, you can provide lots of ways to enrich and enhance his interaction with the world.

As your baby masters his body movements, provide him with lots of challenging gross motor tasks. Babies love to climb, and to solve the problem of getting stuck. Before you know it, your baby will be up in the cookie jar, so lock up your poisons and valuables before he gets into everything. Be sure to let your baby have plenty of time to move around—this is no time for the playpen, except in emergencies, when you can't watch him for a few minutes.

Fine motor development is advancing, too, so provide your baby with things to do with his fingers. He can hold a felt-tip pen like a knife, and he loves to color—on everything! He also likes to pick up tiny objects, so provide him with finger foods he can manage himself. And don't forget the spoon and cup—he's getting better at feeding himself every day.

Thinking skills are in full force as your baby tries to solve his problems, learn how things work, and explore more of his world. You'll hear his first word at one year, if not before, and soon he'll be talking up a storm. Give your baby lots of language input, and play lots of language games to build up his receptive skills and ready him for expressive language.

Your baby has a strong sense of self and knows what's "mine." This is a good thing—he's not being selfish. He's just trying to figure out what part he plays in this world. Use your baby's name a lot, hang his artwork on the refrigerator, give him a mirror in which to look, and watch for his attachment to a special toy. Your baby loves friends at this age, so find him some playmates the same age. Your baby's emotions are fine-tuning, and he's capable of feeling anger, sadness, joy, as well as shame, embarrassment, and jealousy. Allow him to express his feelings and help him with the words.

Don't turn your back! Your baby is on the loose and can't wait to play some of these more advanced games!

BABY-OKEY

Your baby will soon be talking, but before she leaves those funny little noises behind, capture those squeaks and squeals on tape to keep and play back over the years.

Materials:
- Cassette tape recorder and tape
- Infant seat

Learning Skills:	• Language and vocabulary building • Listening skills • Self-identity • Vocalization

What to Do:

1. Insert a fresh tape into a portable tape recorder.

2. Seat your baby in her infant chair and sit down beside her.

3. Turn on the tape recorder and talk to your baby, make mouth noises, vocalize in a variety of ways, and so on, to get your baby to talk back.

4. Pause between your vocalizations so your baby has a chance to answer you.

5. After you've both made some funny noises, turn off the recorder and play back the tape for your baby.

6. Save the tape and play it back when your baby is grown. (Maybe in the presence of her boyfriend!)

Variation: Play a simple baby song and sing along with it. Encourage your baby to join in, and tape the duet. Play back the song when the concert is finished.

Safety: Don't play back the sound too loudly, to protect your baby's hearing.

BELLS ARE RiNGiNG

In this musical version of hide-and-seek, your baby has to search for and find the hidden bells. It's not very difficult—all he has to do is listen while the bells are ringing to discover the secret hiding place.

Materials:
- Soft toy with a bell inside, or a bracelet made of bells
- Various hiding places, such as pillows, soft toys, and blankets

Learning Skills:	• Cause and effect
	• Cognitive development
	• Listening skills

What to Do:

1. Find a toy with a bell, or make a bracelet with bells. (Bigger bells are safer and easier to grasp.)

2. Set your baby on the floor and surround him with a variety of potential hiding places, such as pillows, soft toys, and blankets.

3. Hold up the bells for your baby to see, and shake them for your baby to hear.

4. Secretly hide the bells under or in one of the hiding places.

5. Ask your baby, "Where are the bells?"

6. One by one, lift the hiding objects and shake them. When you lift the object that hides the bells, shake it, but don't let your baby see the bells.

7. Watch your baby's expression change as you shake the bells.

8. Uncover the bells and say, "There are the bells!"

9. Play again, varying the hiding places.

Variation: Hide the bells around the room, then get down on your hands and knees and go exploring. Rattle items as you come to them until you find the bells.

Safety: Be sure the bells are securely attached to something, so your baby can't swallow them.

CATCH THE FIREFLY

As your baby becomes more mobile, she likes to play games of chase and catch. Here's a game that will keep your baby moving as she tries to catch the "firefly" on the bedroom wall.

Materials:
- Cardboard
- Scissors
- Flashlight
- Tape
- Dark room

Learning Skills:	• Cause and effect • Locomotion and coordination • Motor control

What to Do:

1. Cut out a bug shape, such as a firefly, from cardboard, small enough to fit over the lens of the flashlight.

2. Secure the stencil over the flashlight with tape.

3. Make yourself and your baby comfortable in a bedroom and turn off the lights.

4. Turn on the flashlight and shine it at the wall next to your baby.

5. Move the light slowly along the wall, to attract your baby's attention.

6. Tell your baby to go get the firefly that's buzzing around the wall.

7. Move the light slowly away as your baby approaches it and tries to catch it.

Variation: Let your baby "catch" the firefly once in a while by turning off the light for a second, then shine it somewhere else to introduce another firefly. Let your baby operate the flashlight, too.

Safety: Reassure your baby if she gets scared in the dark.

FINGER FRIENDS

At the same time your baby gains control over his large muscles, he also acquires the ability to master his small muscles—specifically, his fingers. Play a game of Finger Friends for finger fun.

Materials:
- Clean, light-colored knit glove
- Permanent felt-tip pens
- Scissors

Learning Skills:	• Fine motor development • Language development • Social interaction

What to Do:

1. Find a clean, light-colored glove that fits snugly.

2. Draw funny faces on the fingertips with permanent felt-tip pens. The faces can represent anyone you like—mom and dad, sister and brother, baby, other favorite relatives, the family pet, and so on.

3. Use scissors to cut the fingers off the gloves.

4. Slip each Finger Friend onto a finger, and give your baby a puppet show, sing some songs, and do some fingerplays, such as "Where Is Thumbkin?"

"Where Is Thumbkin?"
Where is Thumbkin? Where is Thumbkin? (hide thumbs)
Here I am! Here I am! (bring out each thumb)
How are you today, sir? (one thumb bows to the other)
Very fine, I thank you! (the other thumb bows back)
Run away! Run away! (both thumbs disappear again)
(Repeat for Pointer, Tall Man, Ring Man, and Baby, but call them by family names, such as Mom, Dad, Brother, Sister, and Baby.)

Variation: Slip the Finger Friends on your baby's fingers, and let him explore them.

Safety: Be sure that your baby doesn't put the puppets in his mouth—he can choke on them.

FINGERS, TOES, HAIR, AND NOSE

To acquaint your baby further with her body parts, play this simple singing game. It will keep your baby on her toes, while she tries to find her nose! And you can create more lyrics for more body parts.

Materials:
- Floor or infant seat
- Your voice

Learning Skills:	• Gross and fine motor development • Learning body parts • Language development

What to Do:

1. Dress your baby in just a diaper.

2. Seat your baby on the floor or in her infant seat, and sit facing her.

3. Sing the following song, and move your baby's finger to the appropriate body parts.

Put Your Finger in the Air
Put your finger in the air, in the air,
Put your finger in the air, in the air,
Put your finger in the air, then put it in your hair,
Put your finger in your hair, in your hair.
Put your finger on your nose, on your nose,
Put your finger on your nose, on your nose,
Put your finger on your nose, then put it on your toes,
Put your finger on your toes, on your toes.
(repeat with arm/leg, cheeks/chin, lip/hips, neck/back, then)
Put your finger on your finger, on your finger,
Put your finger on your finger, on your finger,
Put your finger on your finger, and then in your lap,
At the end of the song, give a clap!

Variation: Substitute elbow, knee, hand, or foot, or other body parts for finger.

Safety: Play gently so your baby enjoys playing with her fingers and doesn't get hurt.

NESTING BOWLS

At this stage, your baby is trying to figure out how the world works. Nesting Bowls is a game you can play together in the kitchen. While you make your baby a snack, he can practice his new skills!

Materials:
- 3 or more plastic bowls of various sizes that fit inside each other
- 1 square or rectangular plastic pan

Learning Skills:	• Cause and effect • Cognitive development • Gross and fine motor development • Seriation—putting things in order

What to Do:

1. Set three or more plastic bowls on the kitchen floor, already nested inside one another. Set a square or rectangular pan aside, out of sight.

2. Seat your baby on the kitchen floor next to the bowls.

3. Show your baby how to take out the bowls, then how to stack them again according to size.

4. Let your baby have some time to explore the bowls, figure out how they go together, and enjoy the experience of taking them apart and putting them back together.

5. When your baby has figured out how the bowls go together, take them apart and add a square pan to the mix. See what he does with the odd object.

Variation: If you like, buy a set of nesting blocks or bowls at the toy store. For an added surprise, offer your baby a set of Russian nesting dolls, so that each time he pulls apart a doll, another one is inside! You can also do this with boxes, for a homemade nesting toy.

Safety: Be sure to provide plastic items, not glass or metal, so your baby doesn't get hurt. If you use wooden nesting dolls, be careful that your baby doesn't break them, get a splinter, or put them in this mouth.

OVER THE RiVER

During this period, your baby really gets moving. First she begins to creep, then crawl, then walk—and then there's no stopping her. Set up an obstacle course so your baby can use her problem-solving skills.

Materials:
• Small obstacles, such as pillows, blankets, dolls, stuffed animals, blocks, boxes, chairs, tables, and so on

Learning Skills:	• Exercise and coordination • Gross motor development • Problem solving

What to Do:
1. Set up an obstacle course by placing small, soft, pliable, and easily maneuverable objects along a path in the hallway or a small room:

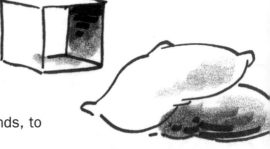

   • Set out a row of pillows for climbing.
   • Spread a blanket loosely over the floor for crawling.
   • Pile up dolls and stuffed animals through which your child can climb.
   • Arrange a small barricade of blocks to challenge her path.
   • Set up large boxes, open at both ends, to serve as tunnels.
   • Place an overturned chair or a small table in the center of the path.

2. Place your baby at one end of the hallway and stand at the other end, making sure your baby can see you.

3. Call to your baby and have her creep, crawl, or walk from one end of the obstacle course to the other.

4. Give lots of encouragement along the way. Offer hints verbally and physically if your baby has difficulty overcoming an obstacle. Move obstacles as needed if your baby gets stuck.

5. When your baby arrives at the other end, give a cheer.

Variation: When your baby completes the course, rearrange the obstacles in a new way and play again. Keep obstacles few and simple in the beginning, then increase difficulty as your baby develops. Include obstacles she has to climb over, squeeze through, jump in, wiggle around, and so on.

Safety: Do not use any objects with sharp corners or hard surfaces, especially if the baby will have contact with the object. (For example, a chair or table may be okay as long as the baby simply has to pass under it—not over.)

PUFF 'N' STUFF

It's time to practice for that first birthday! Prepare your baby for the important task of blowing out his first birthday candle with a game of Puff 'n' Stuff.

Materials:
- Small items that can easily be blown, such as a cotton ball, feather, piece of tissue, corn flake, tiny marshmallow, thistle, and so on
- Plastic straw
- Highchair and tray

Learning Skills:	• Cause and effect • Exploration of weights and properties • Mouth and breath control

What to Do:

1. Seat your baby in his highchair, with the tray secured.

2. Place one lightweight and blowable item on the tray.

3. Blow on the object to show your baby how it can move.

4. Let your baby imitate you.

5. When your baby successfully blows off one of the items, replace it with a new item and try again.

6. Once your baby masters mouth blowing, give him a straw, demonstrate how to use it, and let him try to blow the item with the straw.

Variation: Place the straw in a cup of milk and teach your baby how to blow bubbles. Or, have a blowing contest: Sit opposite your baby and blow an item toward him. When he blows it back at you, blow it back at him again. Repeat until the item is blown off the tray.

Safety: Make sure your baby doesn't swallow the small items.

PUSH–PULL

To give your baby support as she learns to use her wobbly legs, offer her some push and pull toys. While she concentrates on her new plaything, she will be on her feet, practicing her walk.

Materials:
- To push: toy lawn mower, grocery cart, or baby carriage
- To pull: wagon, mobile toy on a string, or stuffed animal on a leash
- Floor space

Learning Skills:	• Cause and effect • Exploration • Gross motor development • Independence

What to Do:

1. Find some push and pull toys for your baby. You can buy them or make them yourself with a little ingenuity.

2. Clear a large floor area for your baby, preferably with no carpet or with a low-pile carpet, so the pushing and pulling is easier.

3. Since pushing is easier to maneuver than pulling, offer your baby one of the push toys first. Hold her hands to the handles and guide her along until she's ready to take off on her own.

4. After your baby has enjoyed the push toys for a while, introduce the pull toys, which require a different skill. If your baby is still cruising (holding onto furniture as she moves) instead of walking, place the toy's handle in her hand and show her how to move with support from you or the furniture.

Variation: If your baby is not yet cruising or walking, hold your baby's hands onto the toys' handles and move with her. For pulling, loosely tie a rope around her waist, attach a stuffed animal to the other end, and let her drag the toy around as she crawls.

Safety: Spot your baby so you can break her fall, but don't be overly protective, or she won't be able to fully explore what she can do with her body and the new playthings.

SLiPPERY SLiDE

Your baby will soon be walking. Meanwhile, he enjoys doing tricks with his body as he learns to control his large muscles, balance, and coordinate his movements. Make a Slippery Slide to challenge your baby's new skills!

Materials:
- Large cardboard box
- Scissors or other cutting instrument
- Couch, cushions, and carpeted floor
- Duct tape

Learning Skills:	• Balance and coordination
	• Cause and effect
	• Gross motor development

What to Do:

1. Cut open a large cardboard box, then cut it into long lengths. Double the cardboard to make your slide stronger, and secure it with duct tape.

2. Place one end of the cardboard slide at the seat of the couch, and use duct tape to keep it in place.

3. Reinforce the underside of the slide with couch cushions.

4. Place another cushion at the bottom, for a soft landing.

5. Hold your baby at the top of the slide and let him slide down gently, as you continue to hold him.

6. Repeat, holding him each time, until he wants to try it without your support.

Variation: Make a slide from a sheet of clear plastic, so it can be used many times.

Safety: Be sure to spot your baby at all times while he's on the slide.

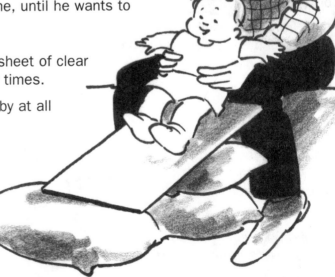

SPAGHETTI WORMS

Babies love gross stuff; they love to touch, squish, and eat anything that has an interesting texture. Here's a fun way to let your baby enjoy her senses while she gets some good nutrition!

Materials:
- Cooked spaghetti, room temperature
- Highchair and tray

Learning Skills:	• Fine motor development and grasp • Self-help skills • Exploration of the senses —touch, texture, and temperature

What to Do:
1. Seat your baby in her highchair and secure the tray.

2. Drop a handful of room-temperature spaghetti onto the tray (no sauce).

3. Let your baby explore the spaghetti. She may try to pick them up, pinch them, squish them, smash them, pound them, grasp them, and finally put them in her mouth.

4. If she starts to throw the spaghetti, redirect her to dropping them on the tray.

Variation: Try a variety of pastas, such as rigatoni, macaroni, wagon wheels, manicotti, or lasagna noodles.

Safety: Keep an eye on your baby to make sure she doesn't put too much in her mouth at once.

SPONGY SHAPES

Water play is fun at any age. Enhance this wet and wild time with Spongy Shapes, which are colorful, creative, and fun to use in the bath—and they're easy to make!

Materials:
- Package of colorful sponges
- Scissors
- Bathtub full of water

Learning Skills:	• Colors and shapes • Sensory stimulation • Social interaction

What to Do:

1. Cut colorful sponges into basic shapes, such as circles, squares, rectangles, and triangles.

2. Fill a tub with warm water and seat your baby inside.

3. Drop sponges into the water and let your baby explore them.

4. After your baby has enjoyed the sponges, take a sponge and press it to the inside of the tub. As you press most of the water out of the sponge, it will stick to the tub, as if by magic.

5. Attach more sponges to the side of the tub, and let your baby pull them off.

6. Talk about the shapes as you play with them.

Variation: Cut the sponges into animal shapes or alphabet letters.

Safety: Do not leave your baby unattended in the tub, and make sure the water temperature is always comfortable.

STICKY TOYS

Now that your baby has mastered the skill of picking up her toys, challenge her by making that task a little more difficult. See if she can figure out how to solve her problem!

Materials:
- Clear Contact paper
- Variety of small toys

Learning Skills:	• Cause and effect • Gross and fine motor development • Problem solving

What to Do:

1. Cut off a length of clear Contact paper, about two feet long.

2. Peel off the protective back layer.

3. Place the Contact paper, sticky-side up, on the floor.

4. Set a number of small toys, such as a block, a plastic doll, a cardboard book, a puzzle piece, and so on, on the sticky paper.

5. Bring your baby over to the toys and set her down nearby.

6. Try to lift a toy from the paper and show your baby that you are having trouble. Ask for help.

7. Watch your baby as she tries to figure out what is happening and how to get the toys off the paper.

Variation: Sit your baby in her highchair and place bits of food, such as raisins, cereal, crackers, and so on, on the sticky paper. Have her try to lift them. When you finish playing, let your baby play with the sticky paper.

Safety: Watch your baby with the paper, so she doesn't cover her face with it. Help her if she gets frustrated, and teach her how to release the toys from the paper.

STUFFY SHiRT

While your baby can still be surprised by what seems magical, play a game of Stuffy Shirt to keep him guessing. Where is all that stuff coming from?!

Materials:
- Several long scarves or neckties
- Large, adult T-shirt

Learning Skills:	• Cause and effect • Object permanence • Social interaction

What to Do:

1. Tie several scarves or neckties together to form one long length.

2. Put on a large T-shirt.

3. Wad up the scarves or neckties and stuff them into your shirt, with one end hanging out by your neck.

4. Seat your baby in his infant seat or on the floor, and sit opposite him.

5. Show him the end of the scarf or necktie, and begin to pull it out.

6. When it's long enough to reach your baby, give him the end and encourage him to pull it out from your shirt. Help him if he needs assistance.

7. When it's completely out, play again.

Variation: Put a large shirt on your baby and stuff the long rope into his shirt. Pull an end out from under his shirt, near his tummy, and keep pulling. Encourage him to pull it as well. This time he gets to feel the sensation of the scarves or neckties as they are extracted.

Safety: Watch your baby at all times so he doesn't get the long length of fabric, rope, or string tangled around his body or his neck.

TEXTURE TRIP

Take your baby on a Texture Trip to Sensory Land, and let her explore the wonders of the material world. As she crawls around this new territory, she'll widen her horizons and stimulate her senses!

Materials:

- Variety of textures, such as a terry cloth towel, a plastic sheet, a piece of fake fur, a wool coat, a silky nightgown, a length of foil, a sheet of wax paper, a roll of egg-carton mattress liner, a large paper bag, a sheet of corrugated cardboard, and so on
- Large floor surface

Learning Skills:	• Cognitive and classification skills • Exploration of the senses—touch, texture, and temperature • Gross motor development

What to Do:

1. Find a large floor area and spread the textures next to each other, covering the floor completely, if possible. Place contrasting textures side by side for a more interesting experience.

2. Set your baby on the edge of the textured floor, and move to the other side.

3. Encourage your baby to come to you over the textured floor. Watch her expression as she feels the differences along the way.

Variation: Wrap your baby in the textures rather than having her crawl over them. Let her have time to feel each texture before you remove it and replace it with another. Talk about the textures as you play.

Safety: Do not leave your baby unattended with the materials. She may try to put them in her mouth and choke.

TRANSFORMING TAPE

This silly game will have you both laughing. While you enjoy the funny faces, your baby will learn all sorts of development skills. Just be careful your funny face doesn't stay that way!

Materials:

- Roll of transparent tape, preferably the soft kind used for taping kids' bandages (the ¾-inch width works best), or transparent kids' Band-Aids
- Mirror

Learning Skills:	• Emotional expression • Sense of humor • Social interaction • Touch and body awareness

What to Do:

1. Set a mirror against a wall in the room so your baby can see himself as he plays.

2. Sit, with your baby in your lap, so you both face the mirror.

3. Take a one-foot length of tape from the dispenser.

4. Make a funny face in the mirror and stick the tape to your face to capture the look. Use several pieces if you like, to make your mouth crooked, your eyebrows stick up, your nose flat, or your eyelids droop.

5. Look at your baby in the mirror and say something funny to go with your funny face.

6. Turn your baby around so he can see you, and begin to pull the tape from your face. Let your baby hold the end of the tape and pull it off.

7. Repeat, making a variety of funny faces.

Variation: After you tape your funny faces, do a couple with your baby's face. Or stick a little piece of tape on his arms and legs and let him pull it off.

Safety: Sometimes funny faces scare babies, so be sure to talk to him while you play and to reassure him you're still Mom or Dad. If you put tape on your baby's face, be very gentle, and be sure not to cover his eyes, nose, or mouth. Remove the tape slowly and gently, and watch your baby carefully so he doesn't swallow the tape.

TUBING

Your baby begins climbing about the same time she starts crawling. Challenge her with her first Tubing experience as she practices moving her newly found legs.

Materials:
- Inner tube or donut-shaped swim toy

Learning Skills:	• Exploration
	• Gross motor development
	• Problem solving

What to Do:

1. Set the tube or other swim toy in the middle of the floor.

2. Place your baby inside the tube.

3. Let her explore the tube and try to solve the problem of how to get out.

4. When she frees herself, give a cheer. Let her spend some time exploring the properties of the tube.

Variation: Provide several tubes to explore. For an extra challenge, put one on top of the other and let your baby try to climb out of both.

Safety: If the tube has a protruding valve, tape it down with duct tape so it won't poke your baby. If you baby gets scared inside the tube, show her how to get out. Then let her explore the tube for a while before trying the task again.

TUNNEL CRAWL

Crawling is an adventure for your developing baby, a skill that opens a new world for him as he explores his environment on all fours. Make him a simple tunnel filled with obstacles to challenge him as he enjoys this new experience.

Materials:
- 3 cardboard boxes, large enough for your baby to crawl through easily
- Scissors
- Duct tape
- Stuffed animals, pillows, or a blanket

Learning Skills:	• Exploration • Gross motor development • Problem solving

What to Do:

1. Cut the flaps off all three boxes and tape the boxes together to form a tunnel.

2. Set the tunnel in the middle of the room.

3. Use stuffed animals, pillows, or a blanket to create obstacles in the tunnel (a blanket will make the floor surface a bit slippery).

4. Place your baby at one end of the tunnel, and walk around to the other end.

5. Peer into the tunnel and call your baby, encouraging him to crawl to you. Entice him with a toy if he's reluctant to enter the tunnel.

6. Cheer him on as he crawls through the tunnel to the other end.

7. Repeat, letting him explore and enjoy the tunnel.

Variation: After your baby is comfortable with the tunnel, drape a blanket on each end. Let him figure out how to get out of the tunnel.

Safety: If your baby is afraid to enter the tunnel, don't force him. Leave the tunnel in the room for a while and let him get used to the idea. Then try again. If your baby gets upset when you cover the ends with blankets, remove them.

WHOOPSY-DAISY!

Once your baby learns to build a tower, she will enjoy knocking it down! Have some fun with Whoopsy-Daisy by building with blocks for the human wrecking ball!

Materials:
- Large blocks, store-bought or made from rectangular milk cartons
- Colorful Contact paper (optional)
- Large flat surface

Learning Skills:	• Cause and effect • Cognitive skills • Fine motor development • Problem solving

What to Do:

1. Buy some large blocks or make your own: Collect quart and half-gallon milk cartons, wash and dry them thoroughly, then cut off the ends. Fold in the sides to make squares and rectangles, and tape them closed. Cover the carton blocks with colorful Contact paper, if you like.

2. Set your baby on the floor with the blocks all around her.

3. Show her how to build a tower by stacking the blocks, one by one. Encourage her to do the same.

4. When the tower is tall enough, let your baby push it down!

5. Build it again and again, until your baby gets tired of the fun.

Variation: Stack household items instead of blocks, if you prefer. You can use toys, books, boxes, crackers—anything stackable.

Safety: If you use something other than blocks, be sure the objects aren't too heavy, so they won't hurt your baby when they come crashing down.

ZIP 'N' SNAP

Your baby will soon be doing things for himself, and you can help him learn those self-help skills with a fun game of Zip 'n' Snap. He'll be surprised and delighted as each layer is removed.

Materials:
- Variety of clothes with different closures—buttons, zippers, snaps, Velcro, and ties
- Your body
- Infant seat

Learning Skills:	• Anticipation and surprise • Cause and effect • Fine motor development • Self-help—dressing

What to Do:

1. Collect a number of clothing items with a variety of fasteners.

2. Put the clothing on in layers, one on top of the other.

3. Place your baby in his infant seat, and sit opposite him.

4. Show him your funny outfit, then begin to peel off the first layer. Let your baby help you with the fastener. Make a surprise face after each task is accomplished.

5. Repeat until all the layers are off.

Variation: Instead of dressing yourself, dress your baby, then removing the layers one by one. Or dress a large doll, so you can both work together to remove the layers.

Safety: Keep your baby from getting frustrated by helping him along the way.

TWELVE MONTHS TO EIGHTEEN MONTHS

This age is a turning point for your baby. She's now able to communicate in simple words and to get from one place to another with little help. As her abilities increase, so does her attention span—and so does her demand for more challenges.

Physically, your baby moves around the room, sometimes on wobbly legs, sometimes at high speed. She'll take a few falls and get a few bumps, but don't restrict her movement—she needs to explore and use her full body to do so. If you're overprotective during this time, your baby will miss opportunities to practice her movement skills. However, do keep a watchful eye—this is when your baby can get away from you before you know it!

Give your baby opportunities to color pictures, eat her food, even begin to dress herself. These self-help skills will save you time in the long run, and will make your baby feel competent and confident, which lead to high self-esteem.

Your baby is moving into the Little Scientist stage, where everything becomes an experiment. When she does something that seems foolish, like stepping on a snail or pouring her milk onto her plate (or floor), she is probably simply exploring her world. Try to understand what and how your baby thinks, and you'll see the world from her perspective. This is a very helpful thing to do, since your baby is very egocentric at this age, and has trouble understanding your perspective—or anybody else's for that matter.

Feed your baby new vocabulary words—she's a sponge for language at this age. But keep the vocabulary in context, as you visit the zoo, go shopping, or change her clothes. Don't make flash cards or drill her on new vocabulary—let your baby learn naturally. And if your baby mispronounces words, let it go. Model the correct pronunciation, but let your baby learn to speak without a lot of criticism and interference.

Friends become more important to your baby as she develops her social skills. She'll soon learn to share, to empathize with others, and to attach to a special loved one or friend outside the immediate family. Dolls and other objects provide your baby the opportunity to nurture, engage in dramatic play, and work out emotions.

As your baby expresses emotions, teach her the words to go with the emotions. If your baby can express her emotions with words, she'll be less likely to act out physically. Your baby is taking her first steps to control her behavior, but this skill takes a long time, so don't expect overnight changes.

Get on your feet and get moving! Your baby is already on her way!

BABY'S HOUSE

It's time to move your baby to his own little home-within-a-home, so he can get a sense of his budding independence. The house will soon turn into a fort, a cave, even a space ship, as your baby's imagination grows!

Materials:
- Card table or other small table, or large cardboard box
- Sheet, blanket, or other covering
- Large floor space
- Flashlight

Learning Skills:	• Cognitive/thinking skills • Imagination and creativity • Sense of self, separation issues • Spatial relationships

What to Do:

1. Set up a card table in the middle of a large floor area.

2. Cover the table with a sheet or blanket to form a house.

3. Fold back a corner to make a door.

4. Go inside and bring your baby with you.

5. Close the corner door and enjoy your new space.

6. When baby feels comfortable, leave him to enjoy his house by himself.

7. Give him a flashlight if his new house is a little dark.

Variation: Draw house details on the sheet or box to make it look more authentic. Let your baby set up toys, pillows, or a little chair inside the house.

Safety: Make sure your baby isn't afraid to go inside the house alone. Leave a corner open if he doesn't like the house to be covered completely.

BODY ART

As your baby grows, she gains increasing interest in her body and its many functions. Bath time is a great time to work on body image, as you introduce your baby to bathtub Body Art!

Materials:
- Children's nontoxic body paint, in a variety of colors
- Bathtub

Learning Skills:	• Creativity • Self-awareness • Sensory stimulation

What to Do:

1. Run a warm bath for your baby; make it shallow enough for her to sit in.

2. Place your baby in the tub and let her get used to the water.

3. Open a tube of body paints and dot the color on your baby's arms.

4. Spread the color with your fingers, and encourage your baby to do the same.

5. Add other colors to other body parts—hands, legs, feet, neck, shoulders, chest, and back.

6. Let your baby spread the colors around, then wash them off and play again.

Variation: Get into the bath with your baby and let her spread the body paint on you!

Safety: Be sure to use nontoxic children's body paints. Keep the body paint off your baby's face, and if she tends to wipe her face with her hands, don't put body paints on her hands.

BOX CAR RACES

Your baby is old enough to go for his first spin in his very own Box Car! All you need for his first set of wheels is a big box, a little paint, and lots of imagination. Then it's time to hit the road!

Materials:
- Cardboard box big enough to fit around your baby's torso
- Poster paint or felt-tip pens
- 3-foot length of rope
- Floor space

Learning Skills:	• Gross motor development • Imagination and make-believe • Social skills

What to Do:

1. Remove the top and bottom of the box, leaving the sides intact.

2. Use paint or felt-tip pens to draw car details onto the box; add doors, headlights and taillights, grill, wheels, and so on. Add a face to the front of the car for fun, if you like. Let your baby help you with the artwork.

3. Cut two holes on each side of the box, large enough for your baby to fit his hands through, so he has something to grip.

4. Let your baby step into the Box Car and run around the room, pretending to drive.

Variation: Tie two pieces of rope from front to back to make shoulder straps, so the box will rest on your baby's shoulders and he won't have to carry it. Decorate the box to look like an animal instead of a car.

Safety: Wrap duct tape around the cut edges of the box to make the box smoother and easier to handle.

BOX-IN-A-BOX

Part Jack-in-the-Box, part Guess-What's-Inside, this game will keep baby guessing—and giggling. Be sure you have something special at the end of the game to make the wait worthwhile!

Materials:
- Variety of boxes in different sizes, nesting one inside another
- Small toy or treat

Learning Skills:	• Object permanence • Problem solving • Sorting, classification, seriation (putting things in order)

What to Do:

1. Collect a variety of boxes that will nest one inside another. Try to get very large boxes and very small boxes, as well as everything in between.

2. Place a special toy or treat in the smallest box for your baby to discover at the end of the game.

3. Close the small box and place it in the next larger box; close the outside box.

4. Continue until you've nested all the boxes inside each other, ending with the giant box.

5. Bring your baby into the room and show her the box.

6. Ask her, "What's inside?" and help her open the box.

7. When your baby sees the next box, say, "Another box!" Lift that box out of the bigger box and ask your baby to open it.

8. Continue until you get to the smallest box, then let your baby open up the surprise!

Variation: Have your baby try to put the boxes back together in order of size.

Safety: Make the boxes easy to open so your baby can do the task herself without getting too frustrated.

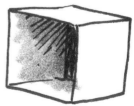

CLIMB THE MOUNTAIN

Most babies, once they get their land legs, like to test them by climbing anything they encounter. Simply walking isn't enough—the kids want to go "up!"

Materials:

- Items to climb, such as sturdy cushions, strong boxes, small stools and chairs, and so on
- Large space to play
- Carpeted floor

Learning Skills:	• Exploration • Gross motor development • Problem solving

What to Do:

1. Arrange items to climb in the play area; leave lots of space between items.

2. Bring your baby into the room and show him the climbing objects.

3. Encourage your baby to climb up, over, and onto the items; help him if he needs assistance.

4. When your baby has conquered each item, place several together so he can climb them all at once.

Variation: Create a stepping-stone type of climbing structure, so your baby climbs up on a cushion to reach a chair to reach the couch. Or arrange the climbing objects in the hallway to create a barrier for your child to climb to get to the other side.

Safety: Be sure to stay with and spot your baby at all times, in case he loses his balance and falls. Cover the floor with blankets and other soft coverings to break his fall.

FIVE LITTLE FINGERS

As your baby learns to control her arms, her hands, and, finally, those tricky little fingers, play Five Little Fingers to help her enhance her fine motor skills. Soon those fingers will do exactly what she wants!

Materials:
- Nontoxic felt-tip pens in a variety of colors
- Baby's fingers and your fingers

Learning Skills:	• Fine motor control • Language development • Social skills

What to Do:

1. Using nontoxic felt-tip pens, draw little faces on your baby's fingers—Daddy, Mommy, Sister, Brother, and Baby. If you prefer, draw facial expressions, instead—happy, sad, angry, sleepy, and surprised.

2. Draw faces on your own fingers to match your baby's fingers.

3. Sit facing each other so you can see each other's fingertips.

4. Sing the following song, and move each corresponding finger. Help your baby move her fingers, too.

Five Little Fingers

One little finger (hold up index finger), *says hello* (bend finger),
Where is my friend? (finger twists)
What do you know! (hold up next finger)
Two little fingers (hold up two fingers), *say hello* (bend fingers),
Where is our friend? (fingers twist)
What do you know! (hold up next finger)
(Repeat for all five fingers.)

Variation: Sing the song first with your own fingers to show baby how the game is played. Then add facial features to her fingers and have her join in.

Safety: Use nontoxic felt-tip pens in case your baby decides to put her fingers in her mouth.

FOLLOW ME!

As your baby moves about the environment, he enjoys a good game of Follow Me! And the best part is, this game is full of surprises, since your baby never knows which way it will go!

Materials:
- Small stuffed animal
- 5- to 6-foot length of string

Learning Skills:	• Exploration • Gross motor development • Problem solving • Visual tracking

What to Do:

1. Find a small stuffed animal that will hold your baby's attention.

2. Tie one end of the string around the animal.

3. Place the animal in the middle of a room.

4. Set the other end of the string out of sight in another room.

5. Place your baby on the floor near the stuffed animal.

6. Move to the other room, out of sight, and pull on the string to make the animal move. Your baby should try to follow the animal.

7. Keep pulling the string, guiding your baby along throughout the house or apartment.

8. After you cover all the rooms, pull up the string to show your baby what you have been doing!

Variation: If another parent is available, have that parent hide and pull the string, while you talk to your baby along the way, saying things like, "There it goes!" and, "Let's follow it!"

Safety: Be sure dangerous obstacles are not in your baby's way, so he won't get hurt. If possible, keep an eye on your baby without him seeing you, to make sure he is safe.

HEAD TO TOES

It's time for your baby's daily workout with a game of Head to Toes, based on a favorite children's song "Head, Shoulders, Knees, and Toes." Only we give the game a new twist!

Materials:
- Colorful stickers or dots
- Body parts

Learning Skills:	• Body parts
	• Gross motor development
	• Movement and coordination

What to Do:

1. Place colorful stickers or dots above your eyes, on your forehead, ears, nose, both shoulders, knees, and all ten toes.

2. Do the same for your baby.

3. Stand up and sing the following song, doing the body movements as you sing:

> ### Head, Shoulders, Knees, and Toes
> Head, shoulders, knees, and toes, knees and toes,
> (touch the stickers on each corresponding body part)
> Head, shoulders, knees, and toes, knees and toes, (same)
> Eyes and ears and mouth and nose,
> (touch the stickers on each corresponding body part)
> Head, shoulders, knees, and toes, knees and toes.

Variation: Dot the body parts with nontoxic felt-tip pens instead of stickers. Add other body parts to the song—arms, legs, chest, neck, hands, feet, back, and bottom.

Safety: Collect all the stickers when you're finished, so your baby doesn't try to eat them. Pens are safer, since then there are no stickers to swallow.

JOLLY JUGGLER

When your baby discovers he has two hands, he becomes fascinated by reaching, grasping, and holding objects. Throw a few things in the air, and watch as your baby becomes the Jolly Juggler!

Materials:
- 3 easy-to-hold, interesting toys

Learning Skills:	• Coordination
	• Fine motor development
	• Problem solving

What to Do:

1. Gather three fun, colorful toys that are easy to grasp and hold. If you have three new toys your baby hasn't seen before, all the better. Keep the toys out of sight.

2. Seat your baby on the floor, or let him stand.

3. Offer your baby one of the toys and let him explore it for a few moments. (Reserve the most exciting toy until last.)

4. As he holds one toy, offer him a second toy for his other hand. Watch his reaction. He may take the second toy along with the first, one in each hand. Or he may release the first toy and concentrate only on the second toy.

5. If he drops the first toy, show him it has dropped and encourage him to pick it up, so that he has a toy in each hand.

6. After he has explored both toys for a few moments, offer him the third toy. Watch your baby's reaction. He may release one toy, both toys, or hold both toys and try to figure out how to take on the new toy! Let him do what he wants to solve his problem.

Variation: Make the game silly by handing your baby more and more toys. Watch them pile up, then all fall down! This should be good for a giggle from both of you!

Safety: Make sure the toys are safe to hold and not too heavy, in case he drops one on his foot!

LISTEN UP!

Increase your baby's listening skills by playing a game of Listen Up! The more noises you provide, the more fun and interesting the game will be, as your baby tries to figure out what makes all that noise!

Materials:
- 3 to 5 (or more) noise-making items, such as a bell, shaker or rattle, bike horn, clicker, stick, squeaky toy, talking doll
- Small blanket

Learning Skills:	• Cause and effect • Listening skills • Problem solving

What to Do:

1. Set three to five noise-making items on the floor in a row.

2. Cover the items with a blanket so your baby can't see them.

3. Seat your baby on the floor near the blanket.

4. Remove the blanket and make a noise, using each of the items, one after another.

5. Cover the items again.

6. Lift the edge of the blanket facing you and make a noise using one of the items.

7. Then uncover all the items and see if your baby can pick out which item made the noise. If she hesitates, make a noise with each of the items, slowly, and see if she can recognize the sound. Praise her when she does.

8. Cover the items and play again.

Variation: Remove the blanket, turn away, and let your baby make a noise using one of the items. Then turn around and guess which item made the noise!

Safety: Don't use any noise-makers that are very loud; you don't want to startle your baby.

"HONK!"

101

MUSIC MAESTRO

As your baby moves about the house, add another dimension to the experience—make your baby's movements musical! Turn your baby into a one-man marching band with a little creative stitching and some bells.

Materials:
- 2 feet of ½-inch-wide elastic
- 10 silver or colored bells
- Needle and thread

Learning Skills:	• Cause and effect
	• Gross and fine motor development
	• Listening skills

What to Do:

1. Wrap elastic loosely around your baby's wrists and ankles, overlapping the ends; mark the length.

2. Sew the elastic ends together to make bracelets and anklets.

3. Sew two bells on each elastic ring, one bell on each side of a ring.

4. Slip the elastic rings onto your baby's wrists and ankles.

5. Shake his arms, then his legs, to make the bells ring.

6. Encourage your baby to walk around, shaking his arms, to make all the bells ring.

Variation: Make a set of musical rings for yourself, and have a parade with the ringing bells. Sew bells around a length of elastic measured to fit around your baby's waist to add to the orchestra.

Safety: Be sure bells are securely attached, so your baby can't swallow them.

PAPER PLAY

There are so many wonderful things for your baby to explore that sometimes we overlook the obvious. A simple sheet of paper can provide your baby with a fascinating opportunity to explore and experiment.

Materials:
- Variety of papers, such as typing paper, stiff tagboard, wax paper, foil, rice paper, colored paper, wrapping paper, and so on
- Floor space

Learning Skills:	• Cognitive skills • Exploration of the senses • Fine motor development

What to Do:

1. Stack a variety of textured papers on the floor.

2. Seat your baby in the middle of the floor.

3. Give your baby one sheet of paper at a time and let her explore the properties of each sheet.

4. When your baby has explored all the papers, show her ways to experiment with them, such as tearing, crinkling into a ball, floating, folding, and so on.

Variation: Cut shapes from the paper and put them together to make pictures and designs.

Safety: Stay with your baby while she plays with the paper, in case she decides to eat it.

POP GOES THE BUBBLE

Just when your baby thinks he's got the world figured out, play a game that will confound him all over again! But don't worry—your baby will have fun, since he will quickly realize what's happening!

Materials:
- Bottle of bubble solution
- Large area for playing

Learning Skills:	• Cause and effect • Exploration • Fine and gross motor development • Social interaction

What to Do:

1. Place your baby in the center of a large room where he is free to move about.

2. Begin blowing bubbles near your baby. (If you like, create your own bubble blower out of a pipe cleaner: Twist the top of a cleaner into a small circle, leaving a little of the cleaner straight to hold when dipping into a soapy solution.)

3. Demonstrate how to chase and pop the bubbles, then encourage your baby to follow your example.

Note: Some babies get very excited during this game and try to pop the bubbles before you've had a chance to blow them. This is a good time to teach your baby patience by waiting a few seconds before you release the bubbles.

Variation: Begin to teach your baby how to blow his own bubbles: Hold the blower near his lips and show him how to blow gently. If your baby has trouble blowing, show him how to wave the blower in the air to make bubbles.

Safety: Watch your baby so he doesn't drink the bubble solution.

SOCK BALL

Get your little one ready for the big leagues with a round of Sock Ball. Sock Balls are ideal for the young athlete because they're soft, easy to grip, and you always have them on hand—or foot!

Materials:
- Large, clean socks, as many as you can provide for the game
- Large bucket, pan, or bowl

Learning Skills:	• Eye/hand coordination • Fine and gross motor development • Social skills

What to Do:

1. Collect a number of clean pairs of socks and roll them into tight balls.

2. Set a large bucket in the middle of the room.

3. Place the balls in the bucket.

4. Have your baby sit one to two feet away from the bucket, and seat yourself next to the bucket. Roll the balls to your baby so she can catch them.

5. When all the balls are out of the bucket, have your baby stand up. Teach her to throw the balls into the bucket. If her aim isn't good, have her come closer and show her how to drop the balls into the bucket. Cheer at every successful shot.

Variation: Instead of throwing the sock balls into the bucket, have your baby throw the sock balls at you!

Safety: If you substitute real balls for sock balls, be sure they are soft and easy to grip.

STRIKE UP THE BAND

Your baby enjoys exploring new sounds, and he especially likes making noises. Here's an opportunity for him to join his first band—and he can play all the instruments!

Materials:
- Noise-making items from the kitchen: aluminum or tin pie pans, pots and pans, plastic bowls, wooden spoons, basting brushes, whisk, empty oatmeal or cereal boxes, empty cans, empty milk cartons, spoons, plastic cups, and jars of seeds or beans
- Kitchen floor

Learning Skills:
- Cause and effect
- Fine and gross motor development
- Listening skills
- Rhythm and movement

What to Do:

1. Collect a number of noise-making items from the kitchen and place them on the floor.

2. Seat your baby in the middle of the kitchen instruments and let him explore their properties.

3. Teach your baby how to make a variety of sounds—pound, tap, beat, shake, rattle, even roll.

4. After your baby has some fun with the instruments, turn on some music and teach him how to keep rhythm.

Variation: Provide your baby with toy-store instruments, such as a tiny piano, small drum set, little guitar, kazoo or harmonica, bells and triangles, even sand paper and sticks.

Safety: Be sure all kitchen items are safe for playing—no sharp edges or corners.

SURPRISE STRING

This game has a dual purpose—it keeps your baby occupied if you're busy, and it teaches her something as she plays! And this game contains a surprise element, which will keep your baby fascinated for a long time.

Materials:
- 4 small toys
- 4 yards of colorful ribbon, rope, or string, cut into yard lengths
- Duct tape
- Highchair

Learning Skills:	• Cause and effect • Increased attention span • Problem solving • Self-help skills

What to Do:

1. Tie one end of ribbon to a small toy. Repeat for remaining toys and ribbons.

2. Use duct tape to attach the free ends of the ribbons to the highchair tray at four different points.

3. Place your baby in the highchair and secure the tray.

4. Let her investigate the ribbons before you show her what to do.

5. After a few minutes, if she hasn't already pulled up the ribbon, show her how to pull it up, then give a surprised cheer when the toy arrives.

6. Let your baby figure out what to do with the other ribbons.

7. When your baby has all four toys, push them off the tray and let her play again.

Variation: Instead of a toy, tie a piece of food to the ribbon, such as a cracker, and let your baby eat the food when she pulls it up onto the tray.

Safety: Be sure to stay with your baby at all times, to ensure that she doesn't get tangled in the ribbon.

TALK TO THE HAND

You've heard the popular expression "Talk to the hand." Take that instruction literally with this game, which helps beginning talkers expand their language skills. Talking is more fun when you have an interesting hand as your conversation partner!

Materials:
- 2 clean, white socks, baby's size
- 2 clean, white socks, parent's size
- Permanent felt-tip pens in a variety of colors
- Wiggly eyes, yarn, felt scraps, and other decorative items
- Glue gun or needle and thread
- Infant seat or floor

Learning Skills:	• Fine motor development
	• Language development
	• Social interaction

What to Do:

1. Use colorful, permanent felt-tip pens to decorate a pair of baby socks and a pair of adult socks with funny faces, turning the socks into monsters, animals, or Muppets. Use the heel as the mouth area and the toe as the nose area, and place the eyes on top of the toes.

2. For more detail and a 3-D look, glue or sew on wiggly eyes, felt tongue and mouth, yarn hair, and other details.

3. Seat your baby in his infant seat or on the floor.

4. Slip the baby socks over his hands and the adult socks over your hands.

5. Let your puppet hands have a conversation with your baby's puppet hands, using interesting topics, simple sentences, and new vocabulary words.

Variation: Seat your baby in his infant seat and use your sock puppets to put on a puppet show for him.

Safety: Make sure all added details are securely fastened, so they don't come loose and wind up in your baby's mouth.

TUBE TALK

Your baby's language skills increase rapidly during this period, from a single word at one year, to nearly fifty by eighteen months. Have fun with speech and vocalization by playing a game of Tube Talk.

Materials:

- 2 paper-towel or toilet-paper tubes, or 1 wrapping-paper tube, cut in half
- Nontoxic felt-tip pens in a variety of colors
- Your voices

Learning Skills:	• Articulation and speech improvement • Language development • Listening skills

What to Do:

1. Decorate the cardboard tubes with nontoxic felt-tip pens to make them attractive, colorful, and fun. Let your baby help.

2. Hold one tube to your mouth and talk to your baby. The sound should be amplified.

3. Give the other tube to your baby and let her imitate you. Hold the tube up to her mouth if she needs help getting started. Encourage her to talk into the tube.

4. Use the tube to make a variety of noises and sounds, and encourage your baby to do the same.

Variation: Make your own megaphone by twisting a sheet of stiff tagboard into a cone. Tape the cone closed and talk into the small end. Talk into a variety of tubes and cylinders to make different sounds.

Safety: Use nontoxic felt-tip pens, since your baby will be putting the tube up to her mouth. Be sure the edges of the tubes are smooth.

WALK THE LADDER

Sometime during this period your baby will master the skill of walking. To challenge his new skill, play a game of Walk the Ladder. Your baby will delight in accomplishing this tricky task.

Materials:
- Wooden ladder
- Large floor space

Learning Skills:	• Coordination and balance
	• Gross motor development
	• Problem solving
	• Visual scanning and depth perception

What to Do:

1. Clear a large floor space of all obstacles.

2. Lay a wooden ladder across the floor.

3. Place your baby at one end of the ladder and walk on the ladder to the other end, stepping slowly into each space between the rungs.

4. When you reach the other side, turn around and call your baby's name. Encourage him to walk along the ladder to reach you. While he concentrates on walking through the ladder rungs, don't distract him. He needs to think about what he's doing.

5. When your baby reaches the other side, give him a cheer and play again.

Variation: After your baby becomes good at walking the ladder, place some toys between the rungs, and have your baby retrieve them on his journey.

Safety: Do not use a ladder with sharp metal edges— that is why a wooden ladder is preferred.

WiGGLY JELL-O WORMS

Wiggly Jell-O Worms are a great way to break that old adage, "Don't play with your food!" Why shouldn't your baby have a good time with her meals and snacks? Food should be fun—to smell, taste, and touch!

Materials:
- Finger Jell-O or Knox Blocks (gelatin that has a firm consistency)
- Highchair and tray

Learning Skills:	• Cognitive skills
	• Exploration
	• Fine motor development
	• Self-help skills—eating

What to Do:

1. Make gelatin according to package directions for firmer consistency.

2. Pour the gelatin into a shallow square pan and chill until firm.

3. Cut the firm gelatin into long thin lengths, approximately four inches by one inch, to simulate worms.

4. Seat your baby in her highchair and secure the tray.

5. Flip the pan of worms over onto the tray to set them free.

6. Let your baby explore the worms with her fingers and mouth!

Variation: Add tiny fruits, small chewy candies, or little gummy treats to the tray of gelatin to make the game more fun.

Safety: Make sure the highchair tray is clean, since your baby will be eating from the surface. If adding items to the gelatin, choose those that won't choke your baby when she eats them.

EiGHTEEN MONTHS TO TWENTY-FOUR MONTHS

As your baby changes into a toddler, you will notice a number of physical, cognitive, social, and emotional changes. These new psycho-social skills will lead him to be more self-aware and independent.

Physically, your baby loses that big tummy, his legs lengthen and gain more muscle, and his fat, stubby fingers become thinner and more dexterous, so he can draw designs on paper instead of just making marks. He can run, walk backwards, hop, climb, ride a three-wheeler, and even ski or skate!

As your baby's thinking skills become more logical, he begins to understand how things work. He can classify the things he learns into groups, which leads him to higher levels of thinking. As your baby understands that not all four-legged animals are dogs, and that not all men are daddies, his cognitive world expands, and he becomes capable of learning more.

Your baby becomes very self-aware and has the capability to recognize himself, his toys, his loved ones, and the things he likes. He may even care about how he looks, and want to pick out his own clothes.

Socially, your baby loves having friends. Although they may quarrel frequently, they make up quickly, as well. Your baby gets better at sharing his toys, but more time will pass before he understands this concept completely.

Your baby is better at controlling his emotions, and should now be using words to express his wants and needs. His range of emotions grows, and he begins to understand the concept of "social referencing," which means he looks to adults for appropriate emotional and social responses.

All in all, your baby becomes less of a baby and more of a young child, and now is the time to play a higher level of games!

ANiMAL WALK

Dr. Doolittle sings a song called "Talk Like the Animals," but your baby can "Walk Like the Animals" with a little assistance from you. All you need are a little imagination and a creative step!

Materials:
- Pictures of animals
- Marching music
- Floor space

Learning Skills:	• Creativity and imagination • Gross motor development • Identification and classification

What to Do:

1. Pick out pictures of animals that have a distinct walk, such as an elephant (sways back and forth), a cat (tiptoes), a dog (runs), a snake (slithers), a crane (high-steps), a duck (waddles), a mouse (scurries), a spider (uses all its arms and legs), and so on.

2. Put on some marching music to inspire your Animal Walk.

3. Stand in the middle of a large floor space and show your baby the first animal picture.

4. Then begin to walk like the animal, using your body creatively.

5. Encourage your baby to follow your footsteps.

6. After a few moments, pick another animal and change your walk to suit.

Variation: Before you demonstrate the animal walk, let your baby try to create a walk for the animal. Play follow-the-leader by leading your baby on an Animal Hike, changing your walk every few steps.

Safety: Be sure the floor space is clear so your baby doesn't trip over anything.

BABY BASKETBALL

Ball games aid the development of eye/hand coordination and gross motor skills for both babies and toddlers, and they give your child a satisfying sense of achievement. Try this basketball game for beginners, and who knows where a little practice may lead?

Materials:
- Large, lightweight plastic or foam ball about 12 inches in diameter
- Large basket, tub, or box, large enough for the ball to fit in easily
- Floor space

Learning Skills:	• Eye/hand coordination • Gross motor development • Social interaction

What to Do:

1. Set your basket or other large container against a wall inside or outside the house.

2. Stand your baby about a foot away from the basket and give him the ball.

3. Encourage him to throw the ball into the basket.

4. If the game is too easy for your budding NBA player, have him move back one or two steps. If it's too hard, have him move forward.

Variation: Tilt the basket a little so the ball goes in easier. Make a line with string or tape so your baby knows where to stand.

Safety: If you're playing indoors, be sure the area is clear of valuables that could be broken.

BURIED TREASURE

Here's a game of Hide and Seek, but in this version, what's hidden is not a person, but a treasure, and the pirate gives clues to its hidden location. Just make sure the treasure is something worth finding after all that work!

Materials:
- Small toy or treat
- Room in which to hide the toy

Learning Skills:	• Cognitive development and thinking skills • Language development • Object permanence • Problem solving

What to Do:
1. Choose a special toy or treat for your baby that will make the search worthwhile.

2. Hide the item in plain sight, but slightly disguised, so finding it won't be too easy or too hard.

3. Bring your baby into the room and tell her you've hidden a treasure.

4. Give her clues by saying, "You're getting closer," or, "You're getting farther."

5. When your baby finds the item, hide it again and again until she gets tired of the game. Or hide a different item each time to hold her interest longer.

Variation: Let your baby be the pirate and hide the toy for you to find. Be sure not to find the treasure too quickly!

Safety: Make sure the room is safe, so your baby won't get into anything that will break or hurt her as she plays.

COOKIE COOK

The kitchen offers a variety of ways to teach your baby a number of skills—everything from language development, to motor skills, to cognitive growth. Let your baby help you cook his first cookie!

Materials:
- Refrigerator cookie dough
- Rolling pin
- Flour
- Cookie cutters
- Cookie sheet
- Candy sprinkles
- Oven

Learning Skills:	• Cognitive skills • Fine motor development • Language development • Math and science

What to Do:

1. Roll out refrigerator cookie dough on a lightly floured surface. Let your baby do some rolling, too.

2. Offer your baby cookie cutters and show him how to press them into the dough.

3. Place the cut-out cookies on a cookie sheet.

4. Let your baby sprinkle the cookies with candy decorations.

5. Bake according to package directions; remove and allow to cool.

6. Eat your cookies with a glass of milk!

Variation: Offer your baby some tubes of frosting and let him squeeze colorful designs onto the baked cookies before he eats them.

Safety: Watch your baby in the kitchen at all times to make sure he doesn't cut, prick, or burn himself.

CREEPY CRAWLER

Once in a while your baby will revert back a stage: Even though she's able to walk well, she may prefer the security of crawling again. When that happens, get on your hands and knees and join your baby in a game of Creepy Crawler.

Materials:
- Pillows, cushions, stuffed animals, blankets, and other soft obstacles
- Large floor space

Learning Skills:
- Dealing with excitement and fear
- Gross motor development
- Problem solving
- Social interaction

What to Do:

1. Fill a large floor space with soft obstacles to challenge your crawler.

2. Place your baby on her hands and knees at one side of the room.

3. Get on your hands and knees behind her.

4. Say, "Here comes the Creepy Crawler," then start to chase her on your hands and knees.

5. Encourage your baby to crawl away.

6. Continue to chase her and watch as she maneuvers around the obstacles in an effort to get away.

7. When she gets tired of playing, reverse the rolls and let her chase you!

Variation: Set up a safe area for your baby, such as a blanket, where the Creepy Crawler can't touch her. When your baby is in her safe area, move away so she has a chance to venture outside the safe area, then give chase again.

Safety: Don't be too scary or your baby will become frightened and not enjoy the game.

DANCING BABY

Your baby has rhythm! All you have to do is turn on the music and he turns on the dancing. So get out on the dance floor and join him for Dancing Baby fun!

Materials:
- Cassette or CD player
- Danceable music
- Floor space

Learning Skills:	• Coordination and balance • Listening skills • Motor movement • Social interaction

What to Do:

1. Select a variety of dance music, such as Raffi tunes, classical, rock and roll, hip-hop, and show tunes.

2. Bring your baby into the middle of the floor and turn on the music. Let him dance any way he wants, letting the music guide his rhythm.

3. Switch music and see how your baby changes his dancing to adjust to the new tune.

4. After a few minutes of dancing, play a game. Explain to your baby that when you turn the music off, everyone must freeze. Then turn on the music and dance together. Every so often, turn off the music and enjoy each other's goofy posture.

5. Continue dancing to different kinds of music, making up dances as you go.

Variation: Clap or stomp along to the music to keep the beat. Sing along with the songs while you dance. Videotape the dancing and show it to your baby when you're finished.

Safety: Make sure the floor isn't too slick; you don't want your baby to slip and fall. You may want to have your baby dance barefoot, for better traction.

DRESS DADDY

Your baby can tell the difference between men and women, boys and girls—mostly by the way they dress. Here's a chance for your baby to Dress Daddy for a change, while she learns how to sort clothing.

Materials:
- Pile of clean laundry that includes a complete outfit for Dad, as well as a variety of other clothes
- Large floor surface

Learning Skills:	• Classification and sorting
	• Fine motor development
	• Gender differences
	• Sequencing

What to Do:

1. Spread out the assorted clothes on the bed or floor.

2. Tell your baby you want to Dress Daddy and that you need help. Ask your baby to choose the first item of clothing. Encourage her to find something of Dad's to begin the dressing, such as his boxer shorts, his socks, or his undershirt.

3. Have your baby continue to locate the appropriate clothes for Daddy, and lay them out on the floor as if dressing him.

4. Be sure you keep things in order, with the undershirt under the main shirt, and the shirt above the pants. Make corrections when needed.

5. When Daddy is dressed, play again and Dress Mommy.

Variation: If you have a large doll, have your baby actually dress the doll using her baby clothes.

Safety: Watch out for loose buttons, tricky zippers, and open pins that might hurt your baby as she plays the game.

FROZEN FUN

As your baby grows and developments, he enjoys the properties of water in many creative ways—in a bowl, from a hose, or in a bathtub.

Materials:
- Ice cube tray
- Small plastic figurines
- Freezer
- Bathtub

Learning Skills:	• Cause and effect • Exploration • Motor development

What to Do:

1. Place small plastic figures into an ice cube tray.

2. Fill tray with water and freeze.

3. Fill a bathtub with warm water.

4. Place your baby in the bathtub.

5. Drop the filled ice cubes into the bath.

6. Let your baby explore the properties of the ice in the water and help him try to figure out what happens as the ice melts.

Variation: Use pint-sized milk cartons to hold larger toys. Tint the ice cubes with food coloring for added fun.

Safety: Keep the water warm enough for baby. You may have to add more warm water as the ice cools the water temperature. Watch your baby in the bath at all times.

GHOST FINGER

What's that scary looking thing in your hand? It's a Ghost Finger! It's come to entertain your baby with fingerplays and conversation. And you don't even have to wait until Halloween to play this game!

Materials:
- White tissue or handkerchief
- Rubber band or string
- Felt-tip pen
- Finger

Learning Skills:	• Creativity and imagination • Finger motor development • Social interaction

What to Do:

1. Place the tip of your index finger in the center of a white tissue or handkerchief.

2. Wrap the tissue or handkerchief around your finger and secure with a rubber band or piece of string.

3. Dot a small face on the tissue with a felt-tip pen; make two eyes, a nose, and a mouth. If you use a tissue, be careful: a felt-tip pen will bleed through.

4. Hold your baby in your lap and bring out your Ghost Finger to get acquainted.

5. Have a conversation with the Ghost Finger; move it around as it responds, to attract your baby's attention.

6. Play "A Little White Ghost," using your Ghost Finger as the song leader.

A Little White Ghost
A Little White Ghost, flying through the air,
(hold your finger up, then move it through the air)
A Little White Ghost, flying through the air,
(repeat)
She flew so high, she almost reached the sky,
(move your finger up high in the air)
But she came back down and said, "Good-Bye!"
(move your finger down, then make it disappear)

Variation: Turn one of your baby's fingers into a Baby Ghost Finger and play together!

Safety: Don't tie the rubber band or string too tightly around your baby's finger.

MUFFIN MIX

If your baby is a picky eater—or a picky person, in general—here's a game that makes it fun to be picky! And this game is tasty, too, since your baby can eat the game materials as you play!

Materials:
- Muffin tin
- 6 types of dry cereals, such as Cheerios, Rice Krispies, Corn Flakes, Chex, tiny Shredded Wheat, and Trix
- 6 bowls

Learning Skills:	• Classification skills • Exploration of tastes • Fine motor development

What to Do:

1. Pour a small amount of each cereal into a separate bowl.

2. Set the bowls in a row on the table.

3. Set the muffin tin behind the bowls, within easy reach of your baby.

4. Place one piece of each cereal into each of the six muffin cups: each cereal should have its own cup.

5. Ask your baby to match the bowls of cereal to the samples in the muffin tin.

6. Have him fill each muffin cup with the matching cereal, using his fingers.

7. Tell your baby he can eat some of the cereals as he plays!

Variation: To make the game more challenging, instead of placing each cereal into a separate bowl, pour small amounts of each cereal on the table and mix them up. Have your baby separate them and place them in the correct muffin tin cup.

Safety: If you use something other than cereal, be sure your baby won't choke on the foods.

123

RAINBOW DOUGH

As your baby's short, stubby little fingers begin to lengthen, they become more adept at doing what your baby wants them to do. Have your baby practice her fine motor skills while she uses her creativity!

Materials:
- 4 cups flour
- 1 cup salt
- 1¾ cups water
- Bowl
- Red, blue, yellow, and green food coloring
- Kitchen implements, such as plastic silverware, rolling pin, cookie cutters, and so on

Learning Skills:	• Cause and effect • Creativity and imagination • Fine motor development • Sensory stimulation

What to Do:

1. Mix flour, salt, and water in a bowl to make dough; knead with your hands until the dough is well blended.

2. Divide the dough into four parts and tint each part with a few drops of food coloring to make one red lump, one blue, one yellow, and one green. Knead until the dough and the coloring are well blended.

3. Seat your baby at the table and place the four balls of dough in front of her.

4. Offer her plastic silverware, rolling pin, cookie cutters, and other kitchen items to help her explore the properties of the dough.

Variation: When your baby makes something from the dough, bake it in the oven at 250 degrees for an hour or more, until firm. Remove the dough shape from heat, cool, and give your baby her new toy.

Safety: Don't let your baby eat the dough.

RED LiGHT, GREEN LiGHT

Just as your baby starts to get going, call out Red Light and make him stop! But he won't mind—you are just playing Red Light, Green Light. And on the Green Light, he gets to go again!

Materials:
- String or tape
- Large floor space

Learning Skills:	• Balance and coordination • Cause and effect • Gross motor development • Listening skills

What to Do:

1. Place a length of string or tape down on the floor at one end of the room.

2. Place another length on the other side of the room, parallel to the first.

3. Clear the floor space between the two lines.

4. Stand your baby on one side of the room and tell him to stay behind the line until you say otherwise.

5. Go stand behind the other line.

6. Tell your baby that when you say, "Green Light!" he must try to get to the other side of the room and cross the other line. But if you say, "Red Light!" he must stop and not move.

7. Play a practice game by facing him and watching him as you call out, "Red Light!" and, "Green Light!" Correct him if necessary and explain the rules again.

8. Once you've had a successful practice game, turn around and face away from your baby. Then call out, "Green Light!"

9. Quickly call out, "Red Light!" and turn around, to catch him if he moves.

10. Keep playing until he crosses the line.

11. Give him a turn to be the traffic cop.

Variation: Play the game with more than one child. Hold up Red and Green signs as you call out, "Red Light!" and, "Green Light!"

Safety: Be sure all obstacles are out of the way so your baby doesn't trip.

SAME OR DiFFERENT?

Your baby's cognitive skills develop rapidly during this time. She now has the rudimentary ability to classify objects based on their similarities and differences. Here's a game that enhances that skill.

Materials:
- Groups of 3 toys, 2 identical and 1 similar, such as playing cards, stuffed animals, blocks, pictures, dolls, plastic food, and so on
- Table

Learning Skills:	• Classification and sorting • Distinguishing similar and different properties • Fine-tuning of cognitive skills

What to Do:
1. Collect items in groups of three. Each group should have two identical items and one slightly different item.

2. Place each group of three in a separate bag.

3. Seat your baby at the table and place one bag on the table.

4. Remove the three items from the bag and set them on the table.

5. Ask your baby which item is not the same as the other two. Let her think about it for a few minutes. If she has trouble, ask questions about the items to help her make the distinction.

6. Bring out the remaining bags, one by one, and let her continue guessing which items don't belong.

Variation: Play the game with food— same and different crackers, cheeses, drinks, candies, breads, cookies, and so on.

Safety: Be sure the items your choose are safe for your baby to handle.

126

SHOE STORE

As your baby teeter-totters on two feet, add a little challenge to the two-step with a trip to the Shoe Store. If you have big feet, no problem—all the better for your baby to walk in your footsteps!

Materials:
- Lots of pairs of shoes, any size
- Socks, optional
- Clear floor space

Learning Skills:	• Balance and coordination • Gross motor development • Matching and classification

What to Do:

1. Select several pairs of shoes from your closet. Choose a variety of styles, including heels, work shoes, boots, sandals, sneakers, and so on.

2. Place the shoes in the center of the room.

3. Let your baby explore the shoes.

4. Mix up the shoes and let him find matching pairs.

5. Then let him put on the shoes and try to walk around.

Variation: Set up an obstacle course for him to maneuver. Have your baby try to walk in shoes that don't match—a boot and a sandal, for example.

Safety: Watch your baby so he doesn't try to put the dirty shoes in his mouth.

SiLLY SHOES

Have a little fun with your baby's new walking skills by playing a game of Silly Shoes. This game will challenge your baby's balance and perception skills while increasing her gross motor development. And it's silly fun!

Materials:
- Variety of fabrics or materials to make into silly shoes—cardboard, felt, fake fur, stiff paper, foam, soft plastic, shoe boxes, and so on
- Duct tape
- Floor space

Learning Skills:	• Balance and coordination
	• Creative thinking
	• Exploration
	• Gross motor development

What to Do:

1. Begin with one of the materials mentioned above, such as a length of fake fur, and wrap it around your baby's feet.

2. Secure the material with duct tape.

3. Let your baby walk around in her new Silly Shoes.

4. Take the shoes off and make another pair using some other material, such as cardboard.

5. Have your baby walk around in her pair of cardboard Silly Shoes.

6. Continue to make shoes and try them out.

Variation: Let your baby come up with her own ideas about making shoes and help her create them.

Safety: Make sure your baby has a clear area to practice walking, without any furniture that might hurt her if she falls.

SPIDER IN THE WEB

Your baby walks all over the place, and loves a new challenge now and then. Make a web for your little spider to follow and watch him figure his way out of the maze!

Materials:
- Skein of colorful yarn
- Large room with furniture
- Transparent tape

Learning Skills:	• Eye/hand coordination • Fine and gross motor development • Problem solving

What to Do:

1. Take a skein of colorful yarn and attach one end to a piece of furniture on one side of the room, at your baby's level.

2. Unwind the yarn as you move around the room, and secure it with tape here and there to various pieces of furniture or tape it to the walls. Make sure the web you create is always at your baby's level.

3. When you've wound the yarn around the room, cut the yarn from the skein, leaving a few feet at the end.

4. Place the end piece outside the room, to lure your baby into the web room.

5. Tell your baby to pick up the end piece and to follow it.

6. Watch him as he follows the yarn through the maze, until he reaches the end.

Variation: Tie little toys to the yarn for your baby to collect as he unravels the maze.

Safety: Be sure to watch him carefully, so he doesn't get tangled up in the yarn.

STICKER FUN

This treasure hunt will have your baby searching right under her nose. With this game of hide-and-seek, your baby's whole body is a winner!

Materials:
- 20 to 30 stickers
- Paper and pencil
- Your baby's body

Learning Skills:	• Body awareness
	• Fine motor development
	• Object permanence
	• Social interaction

What to Do:

1. Buy a variety of stickers that will interest your baby.

2. Write a list of all the stickers so you can identify them.

3. Draw an outline of your baby's body on a sheet of paper, both front and back.

4. Stand your baby in the middle of the room and apply stickers all over her body —some hidden, some in plain sight.

5. Read the name of one of the stickers from the list.

6. Have your baby try to find that particular sticker hidden on her body.

7. When she finds it, have her remove it and stick it in the appropriate place on the paper body outline.

8. Continue until all the stickers have been moved from your baby's body to the paper body.

Variation: Place the stickers all over your body. Then let your baby find all the stickers hidden on you.

Safety: Don't put any stickers in your baby's hair, and make sure to retrieve all the stickers when the game is over.

STREAMER PARADE

You can't keep your baby off his feet during these months, so give him something special to do while he's moving from place to place. Let him lead his own one-baby Streamer Parade!

Materials:
- 1-foot-long smooth wooden or plastic dowel
- 3 yards of crepe paper, ribbon, or fabric
- Duct tape
- Marching music

Learning Skills:	• Balance and coordination • Gross motor development • Visual tracking

What to Do:

1. Find a wooden dowel or plastic stick, about one foot in length.

2. Cut a strip of crepe paper, ribbon, or fabric to three yards.

3. Use duct tape to secure one end of the streamer to the top of the dowel or stick.

4. Give your baby the stick with the attached streamer and show him how to wave it around.

5. Let your baby explore the properties of the streamer, making wide circles, loops, figure-eights, snakes, and so on.

6. When he's ready, play some marching music, and have him march at the head of a one-baby parade while waving his streamer.

Variation: Attach several ribbons to the baton to make a multicolored, multilayered streamer. Join the parade with your own streamer and follow your baby around the room while you march to the music.

Safety: Be sure the stick has no sharp or rough edges, and is lightweight in case your baby drops it. Watch your baby at all times while he's using the streamer so he doesn't get tangled in it.

TOUCH IT!

Parents always seem to tell their babies, "Don't touch!" Here's a chance to say, "Touch it!" instead, with a guessing game that will entertain and educate your baby.

Materials:
- 6 small paper bags
- 6 unusual items to touch

Learning Skills:	• Cognitive skills • Exploration • Mental representation, imagination • Sense of touch

What to Do:

1. Fill each of six paper bags with an unusual item that has interesting sensory properties, such as a Koosh ball, Slime, sponge, wad of cotton, squeaky toy, familiar toy, bottle brush, and so on.

2. Close the bags and set them on the floor.

3. Bring your baby into the room and seat her on the floor next to the bags.

4. Choose one of the bags and open the top.

5. Have your baby stick her hand into the bag without looking inside. Demonstrate with your own hand if your baby is reluctant to explore the contents of the bag with only her hand.

6. Ask your baby what she feels. See if she can guess the item.

7. If she can't, put your hand in the bag and describe the properties of the item to your baby.

8. If she still can't guess, let her pull the item out for identification.

Variation: Place food items inside the bags, let your baby feel them and guess what they are, then let her eat them!

Safety: Be sure the items are safe to touch, with no sharp edges or sticky points.

ZOO ZOUNDS

Your baby rapidly learns about the world around him. Animals are a fun way to expand that learning. Play a game of Zoo Zounds, so your baby can match sounds with the animals!

Materials:
- Pictures of animals that make noises
- Cassette recorder and tape

Learning Skills:	• Classification, sorting, and matching • Exploration • Listening skills

What to Do:

1. Find pictures of animals that make distinct noises, such as a duck, chicken, dog, cat, horse, cow, bird, frog, lion, bear, and so on.

2. Make the sounds of each of the animals, and record them on a cassette tape recorder, pausing between each sound.

3. Sit with baby on your lap on the floor or at the table.

4. Spread the pictures in front of your baby.

5. Look at each picture carefully and identify the animal.

6. Turn on the cassette player and tell your baby to listen to the sound.

7. Pause the cassette player and let baby try to guess which animal made that noise.

8. Continue playing until all the animals have been matched with their sounds.

Variation: If the game is too hard for your baby, play the tape and show him the picture that goes with each sound. Then play the tape again and see if he can remember which sounds and animals match.

Safety: Don't make the noises too loud or scary or your baby will be distracted from guessing.

"MOO!"

TWENTY-FOUR MONTHS TO THIRTY MONTHS

As your toddler passes the two-year mark, she truly becomes less of a baby and more of a young child. She's able to do a number of tasks without assistance (but still with supervision), and has a good grasp of how the world works.

Physically, your toddler's small body is able to do almost as much as an adult body, but without the same strength and endurance. In other words, your toddler gets tired quickly and still needs to replenish frequently with healthy snacks and short naps. Your child wants to imitate Mom and Dad and do grown-up things, so let her have the opportunity to help you out in the yard, the kitchen, and with other tasks and chores. In addition, give your child her own little job to do every day, to give her a feeling of accomplishment and competency.

Around this time, your child learns to control the felt-tip pen, crayon, or pencil, and she's able to make more realistic drawings. Let her have lots of drawing time, with large sheets of paper and large-sized writing instruments. Staying in the lines isn't important at this age, so avoid giving her coloring books, and just let her draw what she wants. Unguided drawing is not only good for fine motor practice, but it is also great for emotional expression.

As your child ponders the things in her environment, she understands cause and effect more clearly, and can figure out how to do more tasks on her own. Let your child try to accomplish tasks on her own, then, if necessary, offer suggestions for solving the problem at hand. Don't try to do everything for your child, or tell her how to do a task "correctly"—give her the freedom to learn how to think for herself. Offer her choices to develop higher-level thinking skills. Encourage your child's creativity and curiosity by asking open-ended questions that begin with "what," "how," or "why," instead of asking "yes" or "no" questions that leave no room for interpretation and exploration.

Language becomes a fun toy at this age, so sing songs, read rhyming books like Dr. Seuss's *Green Eggs and Ham* and Bruce Lansky's *Poetry Party*. Play rhyming games, say silly things, and act out the characters as you read your toddler's favorite storybooks. Provide lots of books for your toddler to "read" on her own. Books offer the opportunity to use imagination, develop language skills, and encourage kids to think.

Your toddler knows what she can do, but she sometimes overestimates her abilities. Try to help her be successful, to maintain her sense of competence. The more confidence your toddler has, the more she will be able to accomplish—now and later. Provide your child with lots of friends, so she learns basic social skills required in group activities. The ability to interact with others will help your child become a better-adjusted kindergartner.

As your child continues to express her emotions, never stifle them, but give her the words to express them. As mentioned above, art activities help a child express emotions that are not easily shared.

Your toddler is two and there's no stopping her now! Just try to keep up with her seemingly limitless energy!

CLOWN'S MOUTH

Now that your toddler's eye/hand coordination has improved, as well as his ability to judge spatial relationships, he is ready for a game of Clown's Mouth. Besides, he'll love being able to hit the target.

Materials:
- Large cardboard box
- Felt-tip pens
- Scissors or X-acto knife
- Crayons, paint, or markers
- Beanbags, sponges, or balled-up socks

Learning Skills:	• Eye/hand coordination • Fine and gross motor development • Spatial relationships

What to Do:

1. Using felt-tip pens, draw a clown face on a large cardboard box. Make two round eyes, large enough to throw a beanbag through, and a round mouth (larger than the eyes).

2. Cut out the eyes and mouth with scissors or an X-acto knife.

3. Color or paint the clown, adding such detail as eyelashes, hair, nose, and so on.

4. Lean the clown face against a wall, and arrange beanbags, sponges, or balled-up socks a few feet away.

5. Have your toddler stand next to the beanbags and other throwing items and try to toss them into the clown's mouth.

6. When he gets good at that, have him try to throw the items through the eyes.

Variation: Make five holes, all different sizes, and let your toddler get points based on the size of the holes.

Safety: Give your toddler only soft things to throw so he doesn't break anything if a toss goes wild!

137

DANCE 'TiL YOU DROP

Most toddlers love to express themselves through music and dance. Provide your toddler with an opportunity for creative body expression, with a fun twist.

Materials:
- Variety of music, such as rumba, waltz, polka, rock and roll, square dance, and so on
- Cassette player
- Large area for dancing

Learning Skills:	• Balance and rhythm
	• Body awareness
	• Creativity
	• Listening skills

What to Do:

1. Tape-record a few minutes of each type of music, allowing enough time to enjoy the tune and do a little dance. Tape one song right after another, so the music plays continuously.

2. Turn on the music and stand in the middle of the room.

3. When the first song comes on, dance to the music, and encourage your toddler to dance with you.

4. When the music changes, change your dance to match, and encourage your toddler to change with you.

5. Dance until you drop.

Variation: Let your toddler lead the style of dance to match the music, and follow her lead.

Safety: Be sure the room is cleared so you don't crash into anything while you're dancing! Take breaks if you get tired.

DRESS-UP PARADE

It seems your toddler can't wait to grow up and be just like Mom or Dad. Give your toddler a chance to practice being a grownup—or at least dress like one—then have a Dress-Up Parade!

Materials:
- Variety of dress-up clothes, such as hats, jackets, gloves, wigs, shoes, pants, tops, dresses, scarves, jewelry, and so on
- Large mirror

Learning Skills:	• Gender identification • Self-awareness • Self-help skills—dressing • Sequencing

What to Do:

1. Rummage a thrift store for a variety of clothes that are easy to put on, comfortable to wear, and, most of all, fun to model.

2. Place the clothes in a box and set it in the middle of the room.

3. Let your toddler explore the box of clothes with you.

4. Try on some of the clothes together, then look at yourselves in the mirror.

5. After you're all dressed up, have a Dress-Up Parade and walk around the neighborhood (or inside your home) in your new clothes.

Variation: Provide several variations of one item, such as a variety of hats, shoes, scarves, wigs, and so on.

Safety: Be careful that your toddler doesn't get tangled up in the clothes and choke. And be sure he doesn't mix a plaid with a print—just kidding!

FLANNEL TALE

Your toddler's language and vocabulary are growing by leaps and bounds, but sometimes her words can't keep up with her need for expression. Provide your child with a simple flannel board and let her tell her tale!

Materials:
- 1 yard of black or dark-colored felt or flannel
- Approximately 3-by-3-foot chalkboard, bulletin board, or sheet of sanded wood
- Glue
- Felt scraps in a variety of colors
- Favorite picture books, such as *The Three Little Pigs, Peter Pan, Snow White,* or *Green Eggs and Ham*
- Scissors
- Felt-tip pens

Learning Skills:	• Emotional expression • Fine motor development • Language and vocabulary development • Social interaction

What to Do:
1. Cover a chalkboard, bulletin board, or sheet of wood with a yard of dark felt or flannel. Secure with glue and let dry.

2. Look through a favorite picture book to choose characters to create. Then, cut out shapes for the characters from felt. For example, if you choose *The Three Little Pigs* as your inspiration, cut out three pigs from pink felt, a wolf from black felt, and a sheep from white felt.

3. Add detail to characters using felt-tip pens.

4. Prop the board up against a wall.

5. Sit with your toddler facing the board, and place the felt characters on the board.

6. Tell the story that goes with the characters, moving the felt characters as you go.

Variation: Cut out any shapes you like from felt and let your toddler place them on the board in any design she wants.

Safety: Be sure the board is secure so it doesn't fall over on your toddler.

GLAD, SAD, AND MAD

Your toddler began experiencing emotions the moment he was born—if not before. Some of the emotions he experienced first are distress, surprise, even anger. This game will help your toddler explore all his feelings.

Materials:
- Paper plates
- Felt-tip pens
- Tongue depressors (optional)
- Cellophane tape
- Picture book

Learning Skills:	• Cognitive skills
	• Emotional expression
	• Language and vocabulary development

What to Do:

1. Draw a variety of faces on paper plates. Each face should express a different feeling, such as glad, sad, mad, happy, sleepy, scared, and so on.

2. Tape a tongue depressor to the bottom of each plate to make a handle, if you like.

3. Hold your toddler in your lap and read him a story that expresses some emotions.

4. When an emotion arises in the book, pull out the appropriate paper plate face and hold it up to your face.

5. Explain to your toddler what vocabulary words go with the emotion and let your toddler make a similar face.

6. Continue reading the story, holding up faces at appropriate times.

Variation: Hold up the paper faces one at a time and copy the emotion with your own face. Describe what you do while you act out the emotion: When you hold up a mad face, say, "I'm mad!"

Safety: Be careful with the tongue depressors so your toddler doesn't get poked with them. They are optional, so use them only if you want. If not, simply hold up the plates by the edge.

GO TOGETHER

This advanced version of the matching game will suit your toddler's higher-level cognitive thinking skills. Make the game fun by providing lots of interesting things that Go Together!

Materials:

- Pairs of items that go together, such as lock and key, pencil and paper, soap and washcloth, cheese and cracker, sock and shoe, nut and bolt, and so on
- Table

Learning Skills:	• Classification and sorting
	• Eye/hand coordination
	• Fine motor development
	• Thinking skills

What to Do:

1. Collect a number of items that go together, as suggested above. Keep them simple. If you like, provide one or two more complex pairs, to challenge your toddler.

2. Arrange all the items on the table, but do not place any of the matching pairs together.

3. Bring your toddler to the table and show her the items.

4. Choose one item and ask her to find which of the remaining items goes with the selected item. Give her hints if she needs them.

5. When she finds the match, praise her, set the pair aside, and choose another item.

6. Continue playing until all items have been paired.

Variation: After your toddler masters the matching of real items, use pictures for the next game. Pictures not only make the game more challenging, they also offer a wider selection of objects.

Safety: Make sure all the items are safe for your toddler's play.

HiDE THE MUSiC

Your toddler uses his senses to learn about his world. His perception causes a motor response, which leads to higher levels of thinking. This game will enhance your child's two most important senses—hearing and sight.

Materials:
- Musical wind-up toy or a battery-operated cassette player
- Playroom

Learning Skills:	• Gross motor development
	• Problem solving
	• Sense of hearing
	• Sense of sight

What to Do:

1. Wind-up or turn on a musical toy and hide it somewhere in the playroom.

2. Have your toddler come into the room and try to find the toy, just by listening.

3. When your toddler finds the toy, praise him, have him step out of the room, then hide the toy again.

Variation: Let your toddler have a turn to hide the musical toy for you. Hide two musical toys so your toddler has to distinguish between the sounds.

Safety: Don't hide the toy too well—your toddler should be able to find it relatively easily, and without having to climb on or overturn things.

MOMMY, MAY i?

As your toddler's language skills grow, she responds to different types of speech. To a statement, she'll give a response, to a question, she'll give an answer, and to a command, she'll play Mommy, May I?

Materials:
- Rope or tape
- Large cleared area

Learning Skills:	• Gross motor development • Language development • Listening skills • Social interaction

What to Do:

1. Place a length of rope or tape along one side of the play area, and make a parallel line several yards away for the finish line.

2. Place your toddler behind one of the lines, and tell her to wait for your instructions.

3. Go stand behind the finish line.

4. Explain the rules of Mommy May I to your toddler. She must ask permission by saying, "Mommy, May I?" before she follows the command.

5. Give your toddler a command, such as, "(Name), you may take three steps."

6. Wait until she says, "Mommy, May I?" If she says it, you can say, "Yes, you may," or, "No, you may not." If you give her permission, wait until she takes the steps, then give her another command.

7. If she forgets to say, "Mommy, May I?" she must go back to the line and start again.

8. When she finally crosses the finish line, let her be the Mommy.

Variation: Invite other kids to play the game with your toddler. Lay out small treats or toys to collect along the way, to make the game more fun.

Safety: Be sure the area is cleared of obstacles.

PAPER WRAP

Just when your toddler thinks he knows all about wearing clothes, dress him in a brand-new outfit. But this outfit is special. Your toddler gets to take these clothes off in a unique way.

Materials:
- Large sheets of crepe paper or butcher paper
- Cellophane tape
- Mirror

Learning Skills:	• Gross and fine motor development • Problem solving • Sense of touch

What to Do:

1. Purchase enough paper to cover your toddler's body.

2. Stand your toddle in front of a mirror and remove his clothes, leaving his diaper.

3. Wrap the crepe paper or butcher paper around his body, creating a new outfit. Let your toddler watch you work in the mirror.

4. Secure the ends with tape to keep it together.

5. Show your toddler his new outfit in the mirror.

6. Once he's enjoyed his new outfit, ask him to figure out how to take it off!

Variation: Try a variety of other papers, such as wax paper, newspaper comic pages, crepe paper strips instead of sheets, and so on.

Safety: Don't cover your toddler's face with the paper, so he can breathe easily and see what's happening. Don't make the clothing too tight or uncomfortable or your toddler won't enjoy the game.

RING AROUND MY TODDLER

This personalized version of Ring around the Rosy will have your toddler exercising her body. Make up your own versions as you play the game!

Materials:
- Large area for playing
- Your voice

What to Do:
1. Dress your toddler and yourself in comfortable clothes.
2. Stand in the middle of a cleared play area.
3. Sing the following song, and act out the instructions as you go:

Learning Skills:
- Body awareness
- Gross motor development
- Language and vocabulary development
- Listening and following instructions
- Social interaction

Ring around My Toddler
Ring around my ... (fill in toddler's name, and move in a circle)
Pocket full of .... (make up any silly word that rhymes with your child's name)
Ashes, ashes, we all fall down! (fall down to the floor)

(For the next verses, substitute, "We all clap hands!" "We stamp our feet!" "We say hello!" "We dance a jig!" "We shake our heads!" "We turn around!" and so on.)

Variation: Personalize any favorite nursery rhyme or song, and add verses that you make up yourself! Try "London Bridge," "Mary Had a Little Lamb," "Tiptoe through the Tulips," and so on.

Safety: Be sure you have enough space to play without bumping into anything. Don't go around too fast, or your child will get dizzy.

146

SCRIBBLE SCRABBLE

Your toddler will soon be writing his name, but the first step toward that fine motor control begins with scribbling. Scribbling turns to design, design turns to pictures, and before you know it, he's writing!

Materials:
- Large felt-tip pens
- Large sheets of white paper
- Kid-sized table

Learning Skills:	• Emotional expression • Fine motor development • Language development

What to Do:

1. Place felt-tip pens and paper on the table.

2. Seat toddler at the table.

3. Sit with your toddler and scribble on the paper together. Encourage him to make a variety of marks, such as dots, lines, curves, and circles.

4. Instead of asking, "What is it?" ask your toddler to tell you about his artwork.

5. Try not to make designs for him to copy. Instead, just let him scribble whatever he wants. As he gains control over the pens, his work will probably become more recognizable.

Variation: Use paint and a paintbrush instead of felt-tip pens, or provide materials for fingerpainting.

Safety: Use nontoxic felt-tip pens, and tell your toddler not to put them in his mouth.

SOUND ALIKE

As your toddler's hearing becomes more and more acute and her cognitive skills more finely tuned, she can differentiate among lots of sounds. Test her hearing acuity—the fun way—with a game of Sound Alike!

Materials:
- 10 small, identical containers with lids, such as pill bottles, margarine tubs, small boxes, or paper cups
- 5 items to place inside the containers to make noise, such as rice, beans, seeds, coins, beads, salt, pellets, or rocks
- Table or floor

Learning Skills:	• Differentiation • Listening skills • Social interaction

What to Do:
1. Place items in containers, making pairs of each, so you have two containers of rice, two containers of beans, and so on.

2. If the containers are transparent, cover them with foil.

3. Set the containers on the table or floor and sit nearby with your toddler.

4. Pick up one of the containers and shake it.

5. Have your toddler pick up another container and shake it.

6. Ask if the sounds are the same or different.

7. Keep shaking containers until your toddler finds the one that makes the same sound as yours.

8. Continue playing until all containers are matched, then show your toddler what's inside.

RATTLE!
RATTLE!

Variety: Fill glasses with varying levels of liquid, tap them with a spoon, and listen to the different sounds they make.

Safety: Make sure the containers are secure, so they won't open until you're ready to show the contents to your toddler.

STICKER MAGIC

Combine getting clean with having fun by playing Sticker Magic in the bathtub. Your child will love to see how small characters and shapes magically stick to the side of the tub!

Materials:
- Inexpensive picture book that you don't mind cutting up
- Clear Contact paper
- Scissors
- Bathtub and water

Learning Skills:	• Cause and effect
	• Creativity and imagination
	• Fine motor development

What to Do:

1. Buy an inexpensive picture book that your toddler loves, such as a Disney book, a Golden book, or a comic book.

2. Cut out the characters in the book, and some of the props, if you like. You can cut out several views of the same character, such as sitting, standing, and running. For props you might include furniture, toys, a house, or a car.

3. Lay out a length of Contact paper faceup on the table, with the protective covering removed.

4. Place the figures on the paper, faceup, leaving an inch between each figure.

5. Lay another piece of Contact paper on top of the first, this time facedown, so the figures are encased in the plastic paper. The figures will then be waterproof.

6. Carefully cut around the figures, leaving a one-eighth-inch margin. If you cut too close to the edge of the figure, the Contact paper will not stick together.

7. Fill the bathtub with warm water.

8. Place your toddler in the tub, along with the plastic-covered figures.

9. Press one of the wet cut-out figures to the side of the bathtub and watch it stick!

Variation: You don't have to be in the tub to enjoy this game. Fill a tub of water outside, lower a metal cookie sheet into the tub, and press the stickers onto the cookie sheet.

Safety: Be sure you stay with your toddler while he's in the water.

STORYTELLER

When your toddler likes something, she tends to want it repeated—over and over and over again! Here's a fun way to accommodate her, while enhancing her cognitive skills.

Materials:
- Cassette tape recorder
- Blank tape
- Picture book
- Comfortable area for listening

Learning Skills:	• Language and vocabulary development • Listening skills • Self-help skills—reading

What to Do:

1. Hold your toddler in your lap, along with a picture book.

2. Turn on the tape recorder to record your voice.

3. Read the storybook to your toddler, making sure you speak clearly enough for the recorder.

4. When the book is finished, turn off the recorder and rewind the tape.

5. Place your toddler in a comfortable area and give her the book.

6. Set the tape recorder nearby and teach her how to turn it on, or turn it on yourself.

7. Have her look at the book and turn the pages as the story plays on the tape recorder.

Variation: Make up a story without a storybook, and let your toddler use her imagination to picture what is happening.

Safety: Use a portable cassette recorder made for kids so your toddler can operate it safely.

"THE DUCK SAYS QUACK!"

TASTE AND TELL

Your toddler is eating more foods and trying new tastes. If you have a picky eater who turns up his nose at anything green, try this taste test and turn mealtime into a game.

Materials:

- Variety of your toddler's favorite foods that are similar in texture, such as applesauce, pudding, mashed potatoes, Jell-O, soup, cereal, yogurt, and so on
- Bowls
- Table
- Spoon
- Blindfold

Learning Skills:	• Classification skills • Exploration • Risk taking • Sense of taste

What to Do:

1. Select a variety of foods that are similar in texture, such as the ones mentioned above.

2. Place the foods in individual bowls, and set the bowls in a row on the table.

3. Place your toddler at the table and give him a spoon.

4. Point out all the foods, one by one, and tell him you're going to play a game.

5. Blindfold your toddler or tell him to close his eyes.

6. Take the spoon, fill it with one of the foods, and have your toddler taste it.

7. Remove the blindfold and ask him to guess which food he ate.

8. Repeat until he's tasted all the foods.

Variation: Play the game with just fruits, just vegetables, just cereals, or other categories of foods.

Safety: Don't try to trick your toddler by feeding him a food he doesn't like, or he won't trust you.

TODDLER BOWLING

Instead of having your toddler just roll a ball back and forth, give her an extra challenge by setting up some objects to knock over. Then play a game of Toddler Bowling!

Materials:
- 6 to 10 items to serve as bowling pins, such as empty milk cartons, empty plastic drink bottles, upside-down paper cups, and so on
- Large cleared area
- String or tape
- Volleyball, soccer ball, or basketball

Learning Skills:	• Cause and effect • Eye/hand coordination • Gross motor development

What to Do:

1. Set up the "bowling pins" in a triangle pattern, like pins in a bowling alley.

2. Take several steps back and mark a line with string or tape.

3. Have your toddler stand behind the line.

4. Give her the ball and tell her to try to knock down all the objects by rolling the ball.

5. Let her keep rolling until she knocks them all down.

6. Set them up again and play another round.

Variation: Set a row of dominoes in a long line. Have your toddler roll a small ball toward the first domino, so that when it hits, the dominoes will fall down in a chain reaction.

Safety: Don't use a real bowling ball—it's too heavy for your toddler to handle. Do not use breakable objects as your bowling pins.

TOSS IT!

This is a lively, interactive game, that keeps your toddler moving, laughing, and winning. You play the part of the basket, while your toddler gets to Toss It!

Materials:
- Small balls, such as tennis balls, Nerf balls, or Koosh balls
- Large, lightweight container, such as a bucket, box, or bag
- Large play area

Learning Skills:	• Eye/hand coordination • Gross motor development • Social interaction

What to Do:

1. Collect several small balls and put them on the floor near your toddler.

2. Find a container large enough to catch the balls, and easy to hold.

3. Hold the container in your hands, down at your toddler's level.

4. Have your toddler try to throw a ball into the container.

5. Move the container so you catch the ball. As you work together, the two of you should be able to get all the balls into the container.

6. When all the balls are in the container, give them back to your toddler and let him play again.

Variation: Give your toddler the container to hold, and you toss the balls inside.

Safety: Throw the balls lightly, and be careful not to throw the balls at your toddler's face. Make sure the container doesn't have any sharp edges.

WASH 'EM UP

Unlike Tom Sawyer and his reluctance to paint the fence, most toddlers love to do "real work"—even if it's just pretend. Give your toddler a brush and a bucket of water and watch her clean her world!

Materials:
- Large, clean paintbrush
- Child-safe cleaning items, such as sponges, towels, squeegees, squirt bottles, scrubbers, dust cloths, cobweb cleaners, and so on
- 2 small buckets
- Water

Learning Skills:	• Cause and effect
	• Enhanced self-esteem
	• Eye/hand coordination
	• Gross motor development

What to Do:
1. Collect child-safe cleaning items in a bucket, so your toddler can carry them from place to place.

2. Fill the other bucket with water.

3. Take your toddler outside and teach her how to "paint" the house with the brush and water.

4. Then let her explore the other cleaning items and use them the way she's seen you use them.

5. Praise your toddler on the great job she's done cleaning the house!

Variation: If you're working on a household task, such as dusting or sweeping, think about how you can let your toddler help in some small way, or give her a similar project she can do on her own.

Safety: Make sure all cleaning items are safe to be handled by your toddler. This is a good time to teach your toddler about the danger of poisonous items—in this case, various cleaning fluids.

WHAT'S INSIDE?

Your toddler is often called a Little Scientist at this age, because he's so curious. He likes to take things apart and find out what's inside. Here's a game of What's Inside that will stimulate your budding Einstein!

Materials:
- Paper lunch bags
- Small items to fit inside the lunch bags: special toys, hairbrush, toddler bottle, diaper, ball, doll, set of keys, shoe, and so on
- Transparent tape

Learning Skills:	• Classification and identification • Cognitive/thinking skills • Fine motor development • Problem solving

What to Do:

1. Collect a number of items familiar to your toddler, such as those mentioned above.

2. Place one in each paper bag, fold over the top of the bag, and tape the bag closed.

3. Sit with your toddler on the floor, with the bags hidden behind you.

4. Bring out one bag and let your toddler feel it on the outside. Say, "I wonder what's inside?" as you both feel the bag.

5. Let your toddler make a guess. If he doesn't guess, you can make a guess, but don't guess correctly. This will begin your child's thinking process, as he ponders what could be inside the bag.

6. Continue feeling and guessing. If your toddler gives up, open the bag and let him feel the item without looking at it. See if he can now guess the item.

7. When both of you have finished guessing, bring out the item and see if your toddler was right.

Variation: Let your toddler make a set of feely bags for you to guess!

Safety: Be sure nothing inside the bags could hurt your toddler as he explores them with his hands.

WHAT'S WRONG?

Your toddler is still figuring out how the world works when you introduce a game of What's Wrong? See if she can figure out what's so silly about this game—and how to fix it!

Materials:
- Picture book
- Sock and shoe
- Toothbrush and toothpaste
- Bowl and water
- Cracker and peanut butter

Learning Skills:	• Fine motor development
	• Problem solving
	• Social interaction

What to Do:

1. Collect the items above, or other items that can be turned around, upside down, or made to look different than usual in any other way.

2. Hold your toddler in your lap. Hold a picture book upside down and begin to read. See if your toddler can figure out that the book is wrong and fix it.

3. Put a shoe on your toddler's foot, then put on the sock. See if your toddler notices what's wrong and tries to fix it.

4. Put toothpaste on the back of the toothbrush instead of on the bristles. See if your toddler can figure out what's wrong and what to do about it.

5. Pour some water into a bowl and tell your toddler you brought her a drink. See if she notices the silly container and asks for a glass.

6. Spread peanut butter on a cracker and set it upside down on a plate. See if your toddler turns it right-side up!

Variation: Add more twists to your toddler's everyday life to see if she notices changes and makes adjustments. For example, wear a hat upside down, put on clothes inside out, eat with wrong utensils, tint rice with food coloring, and so on.

Safety: Be sure your toddler can't get hurt doing these silly tasks.

THIRTY MONTHS TO THIRTY-SIX MONTHS

Your about-to-turn-three-year-old is ready to face the world! He's grown into a fit, smart, and self-assured child, eager to join his peers in the preschool class-room or in the neighborhood yard. How quickly he changed from being a dependent baby who didn't talk or walk, to a young child who speaks his mind, does what he wants, and knows himself.

As your child's gross motor skills increase, he'll soon ride a two-wheeler, skate, ski, jump rope, play hopscotch, even ride a skateboard! He can run faster, jump higher, and last longer during physical play.

Your child's fine motor skills also develop rapidly. He'll soon write the alpha-bet and his own name, as well as draw intricate pictures with clarity and meaning. He can dress, feed, and toilet himself, and these self-help skills lead to a feeling of independence and competence.

Your child loves to ask questions, especially, "Why?" as he pieces together the puzzles of his environment. He can follow simple instructions, think things through to some degree, and figure out most of his own problems.

His language skills are remarkable—he learns six to ten new words a day! Some of that vocabulary will surprise you, too, as he suddenly uses words and phrases like, "That's despicable!" or, "I'm feeling very angry today!" If your child picks up a few bad words, explain that you don't use those words in your home, and ignore them after that. If you don't give your child attention for using those words, they'll soon lose their impact and disappear—as long as you're not model-ing them!

Your child should be feeling good about himself as he learns more tasks and meets more challenges. During the school years his self-esteem may drop a bit, but if it was well-developed during the early years, he'll regain the confidence he once had. Give your child plenty of opportunity to succeed and do things for him-self to strengthen his self-esteem.

As your child learns to reciprocate and begins to understand how others feel, his friendships last longer and his disagreements are fewer. And as his emotions become more complex, your child is more able to express them—through physical movement, language, and art. Encourage your child to express his emotions in an acceptable way, so he develops his own coping skills by the time he grows up.

And speaking of growing up—he is—rapidly! So enjoy the time with your three-year-old. Before you know it, he'll be four!

BAG OF FUN

Surprises are great fun for your toddler, especially when they're creative and open-ended. Put together a Bag of Fun to provide your toddler with stimulating ideas for her imagination.

Materials:
- 4 paper bags
- 3 items that go together per bag, such as soap, washcloth, and plastic boat (for the bath); spoon, plate, and cup (for eating); shoes, shirt, and pants (for dressing)

Learning Skills:
- Cognitive/thinking skills
- Identification and classification
- Language development
- Social interaction

What to Do:

1. Place three items that go together, such as those suggested above, in a paper bag.

2. Repeat for two more bags.

3. Seat your toddler on the floor and bring out the first bag.

4. Open the bag and let your toddler pull out one item, without seeing the rest.

5. First ask her to identify the item, then ask her what else she thinks is inside.

6. If she guesses one of the items correctly, bring it out and show her.

7. Then ask her to guess what the last item is.

8. If your child has trouble guessing the third related item, show her how the first and second items go together. Then have her try to guess the third item.

9. When she has guessed all three items, ask her what they all have in common.

10. Repeat for the other bags.

Variation: Play the game with food. Set three related items on the table, such as a pizza crust or dough, pizza sauce, and grated cheese. Ask your toddler what the food will be when the items are combined.

Safety: Be sure none of the items are harmful to your toddler, and try to select items that are familiar to your child, so she is sure to guess at least some correctly.

COPYCAT

Your toddler is a great imitator—which is one of the ways he learns. Turn the tables on him and play a game of Copycat, where you do the imitating!

Materials:
• Your bodies

Learning Skills:	• Cause and effect • Gross and fine motor development • Social interaction

What to Do:

1. Bring your toddler into the playroom and set him on the floor.

2. Sit down next to him, imitating his exact body position.

3. Every time your toddler moves or does something, do exactly what he does.

4. See if you can tell when he catches on to what you're doing!

Variation: Instead of imitating him, do a task and have your toddler imitate you. For example, clap your hands three times, then tell your toddler to do the same. Continue adding body movements and having your toddler imitate you. Then tell your toddler to lead the body movements and you copy him.

Safety: Stop the game if your toddler gets into anything dangerous and deal with the problem before you continue. Don't tease your toddler or upset him with your imitating.

DINOSAUR DIG

Kids this age love dinosaurs. While they may not be able to pronounce the word spaghetti, the name of Tyrannosaurus Rex seems to come easily. Here's a game for your young archeologist to play!

Materials:
- Plastic dinosaur bones, available at a toy or science store
- Sandbox
- Spoon or small plastic shovel

Learning Skills:	• Cognitive skills (relationship of a part to the whole) • Fine motor development • Language development

What to Do:

1. Separate a set of dinosaur bones into individual parts and bury the parts in the sandbox.

2. Offer your toddler a spoon or a small plastic shovel and tell her to dig in the sand for dinosaur bones.

3. When she finds a bone, tell her to lay it out on the ground, and keep looking for more.

4. After she finds all the bones, work together to put the dinosaur back together.

Variation: You can use any toy that has a lot of parts, such as a puzzle, a construction set, a collection of farm animals, and so on.

Safety: Stay with your toddler to make sure she doesn't get sand in her eyes.

HAT PLAY

Your toddler is developing a vivid imagination and enjoys playing different roles. Provide a variety of items to stimulation his imagination, beginning with a collection of interesting hats!

Materials:
- Variety of hats, such as a baseball cap, straw hat, sock hat, beanie, firefighter's hat, soldier's hat, feather hat, cowboy hat, Stetson, beret, scarf, toddler bonnet, and newspaper hat
- Mirror

Learning Skills:	• Body awareness and sense of self • Dramatic play and imagination • Gross and fine motor development

What to Do:

1. Collect a variety of hats from a thrift shop, the neighbors, or your closet. The more hats you have, the more your toddler can make-believe.

2. Place the hats in a large box and close the lid.

3. Place the box next to a mirror in the playroom.

4. Invite your toddler to open the box and pull out a hat.

5. Have him try it on, then you try it on, and look in the mirror to enjoy your new look.

6. Encourage your toddler to act like someone who might wear that hat. For example, if he wears a baseball cap, he might pretend to swing a bat.

Variation: Do the same with shoes, wigs, clothes, make-up, masks, and so on.

Safety: Be sure the hats are clean and have no hatpins inside!

LAUNDRY LOAD

What may be a chore for you is often a good game for your toddler! Play Laundry Load to help your toddler develop classification and thinking skills—and get the laundry sorted, too!

Materials:
- Large load of the family's laundry, washed and dried
- Clean floor space

Learning Skills:	• Body awareness • Classification and sorting • Fine and gross motor development

What to Do:

1. After the laundry has been washed and dried, pile it in the middle of a clean floor.

2. Seat your toddler next to you and teach her how to sort the laundry based on simple groups. For example, you might sort according to color, with reds in one pile, greens in another, blues in another, and so on.

3. After you've sorted the laundry according to one characteristic, sort it again according to a different characteristic. You might try classifying by size, shape, gender, family member, new/old, or whether the item has fasteners.

Variation: Tell your toddler to close her eyes and guess what pile an item belongs in just by feel.

Safety: If your toddler tries on any of the clothes, make sure she doesn't get tangled up in them.

KNOW THE NOISE

Your toddler loves to listen—to music, to voices, to animals. Enhance his listening skills with a variety of familiar sounds he can guess. All you need is a portable cassette recorder.

Materials:
- Portable cassette recorder and tape
- Interesting sounds

Learning Skills:	• Cause and effect • Classification skills • Listening skills

What to Do:

1. Use a tape recorder to record a variety of interesting sounds, such as a dog barking, *Sesame Street* song, musical toy, Daddy's voice, telephone ringing, keys jangling, and so on. Allow some time between each noise.

2. Play the tape for your toddler and see if he can guess each sound. If you have not left enough time between noises, stop the tape after each noise and allow your child to guess.

3. Play the tape again; this time, demonstrate the source of each noise as it plays.

Variation: Tape-record familiar voices for your toddler, such as grandparents, babysitters, siblings, friends, neighbors, then ask your child to identify the people by voice.

Safety: Be sure the noises are loud enough to be heard, but soft enough to avoid startling your toddler.

MAGIC GLASSES

Although your toddler already sees the world from her own unique perspective—egocentrism—you can offer her another way to see things with these Magic Glasses. Don't we all want to see our world through rose-colored glasses?

Materials:
- Flexible tagboard (or the back of a cereal box)
- Pencil
- Scissors
- Red, blue, green, and yellow cellophane
- Masking or duct tape

Learning Skills:	• Classification skills • Creativity and imagination • Visual stimulation and acuity

What to Do:
1. Cut out a strip of flexible tagboard, large enough to cover your toddler's eyes and long enough to circle her head with a bit of overlap.

2. Hold the strip of tagboard to your child's face and mark the eyeholes with a pencil.

3. Cut out large eyeholes so your toddler can see clearly when she wears the glasses.

4. Cut out a strip of red cellophane, lay it over the eyeholes, and tape it down.

5. Place the mask, tape-side out, on your toddler's face, making sure she can see. Tape the mask together at the back.

6. Let your toddler explore her red-colored world.

7. When she gets tired of red, change the color to blue, then green, then yellow.

Variation: Instead of making glasses, make a telescope! Cover one end of a paper-towel tube with colored cellophane, and let your toddler look at the world with one colored eye!

Safety: Be sure your toddler can take off the glasses easily so she doesn't get scared.

MiX iT UP

As your toddler pieces his world together, play games that enhance his ability to sequence—a skill that must be mastered before he can attempt to learn to read.

Materials:

- Series of photos, such as vacation, birthday party, holiday event, first day at preschool, and so on
- Large sheet of white construction paper
- Felt-tip pen
- Table

Learning Skills:
- Cause and effect
- Cognitive/thinking skills
- Sequencing and prereading skills
- Visual discrimination

What to Do:

1. Search the family photo album for a series of four pictures that focus on a particular event, as mentioned above. Select pictures that have a beginning, middle, and end. For example: 1. Welcoming party guests. 2. Opening gifts. 3. Eating the cake. 4. Saying good-bye.

2. On a large sheet of construction paper, draw a row of four squares, a little larger than the size of the photographs.

3. Label the first square #1, then #2, #3, and #4.

4. Seat your toddler at the table with the construction paper in front of him.

5. Spread out the four photographs for your toddler to see.

6. Remind him of the event, then ask, "What happened first?" See if he can pick out the photograph that represents the beginning of the event. If he needs help, give him clues.

7. Have your toddler set the beginning picture on square #1.

8. Search for picture #2, and continue until all pictures have been placed in order.

Variation: Instead of using photographs, cut up a favorite inexpensive children's picture book, taking a page from the beginning, two from the middle, and one from the end. Have your toddler arrange them in order.

Safety: If your toddler gets frustrated, use only three pictures, and help him with lots of clues.

PAINT WiTH PUDDiNG

Your toddler likes to classify things to organize her world. But some things overlap, and when you present your toddler with new ways of thinking, you enhance her cognitive development. Here's something new!

Materials:
- Pudding
- Table covered with plastic
- Bib or smock

Learning Skills:	• Classification and thinking skills
	• Emotional and creative expression
	• Fine motor development

What to Do:

1. Buy or make pudding in your child's favorite flavor.

2. Cover the table with plastic (or use a table that will wipe clean after use).

3. Cover your toddler with a bib or smock.

4. Seat your toddler at the table in a chair seat, so she can reach the table easily.

5. Scoop a large spoonful of pudding onto the table in front of your toddler and let her fingerpaint with it. Show her how, if she needs some encouragement.

Variation: Use vanilla pudding and tint portions of it in a variety of colors for added visual enjoyment. If you want to save a design, press a sheet of white paper on top of the pudding design, lift it up carefully, then let it dry.

Safety: Your toddler can taste the pudding as she plays. However, when you use inedible fingerpaints, teach her not to taste them.

PiCTURE PAiRS

As your toddler begins to recognize the similarities and differences between the three-dimensional world and two-dimensional representations, such as pictures, play a game of Picture Pairs and see if he can match up 3-D and 2-D!

Materials:
- Pictures from magazines that represent things found around the house, such as toothpaste, toddler food, hat, toy, shoes, watch, and so on
- Real items to match to pictures

Learning Skills:	• Classification and matching
	• Real vs. representation
	• Visual discrimination

What to Do:

1. Find pictures that represent items found in your home, as suggested above.

2. Collect real items to match the pictures.

3. Set out the real items in a row on the floor or at the table.

4. Seat your toddler next to you, facing the items.

5. Hold up a picture of one of the items and ask your toddler to find the matching real item.

6. Repeat until your toddler matches all the items.

Variation: Omit a couple of items so that some of the pictures don't match anything, and see if your toddler can tell what's missing. Instead of matching things that are the same, such as a real toothbrush and a picture of a toothbrush, match items that are related, such as a toothbrush and toothpaste.

Safety: Be sure all items are safety for your toddler to handle, and give him lots of praise, encouragement, and help so he doesn't become frustrated.

SAND AND WATER

Sand and water are two properties that offer your toddler a wide range of open-ended activities. All she needs are a box of sand and pail of water to pretend she's at the beach, as she pours, presses, molds, and sifts.

Materials:
- Large wooden or cardboard box
- Fine sand
- Bucket of water
- Sand toys, plastic animals, small figures
- Sifters, cups, scoops, spoons, and other kitchen items

Learning Skills:	• Cause and effect • Fine motor development • Imagination and dramatic play • Sensory exploration

What to Do:

1. Set a large wooden or cardboard box in the yard and fill it at least one-foot deep with fine sand.

2. Set out a bucket of water, sand toys, and kitchen items for discovery play.

3. Let your toddler enjoy exploring the sand and using her imagination as she sifts, pours, buries, and plays.

Variation: Bury some small toys in the sand when your toddler isn't looking, and let her discover the hidden treasures.

Safety: Watch your toddler around the sand, in case she gets it in her face.

SHELL GAME

Can you fool your toddler? When he was younger you could, but now that he's growing up, it won't be so easy. Still, don't let him bet his future college fund on this Shell Game!

Materials:
- Table
- 3 small cups or bowls in different colors
- Bite-sized candies, cookies, or crackers

Learning Skills:	• Eye/hand coordination • Problem solving • Visual acuity and tracking

What to Do:

1. Seat your toddler at the table.

2. Place three colored bowls on the table, facedown.

3. Set a bite-sized candy, cookie, or cracker in front of one of the bowls.

4. Cover the treat with a bowl.

5. Move the bowls around, keeping your toddler's attention on the hidden treat.

6. Ask you toddler, "Where's the treat?"

7. Let your toddler pick up the bowl to check for the treat.

8. If he guesses correctly, let him eat the treat.

9. Play again!

Variation: Put treats under all three bowls and ask him to find the treat you select. To make the game more challenging, play with three bowls of the same color.

Safety: Move the bowls slowly, so your toddler can track the treat. The idea here is to make him successful, not to frustrate him.

SiLLY STORiES

Just when your toddler thinks she's got the world figured out, tell her a Silly Story and make her think again! This fun game requires the use of your toddler's favorite storybooks.

Materials:
• Favorite picture book

Learning Skills:	• Cognitive/thinking skills
	• Language and vocabulary development
	• Social interaction

What to Do:

1. Select one of your toddler's favorite picture books—one that you read to her frequently.

2. Sit with your toddler on your lap in a comfortable place.

3. Begin to read the book to your toddler, as you always have.

4. After a few pages, instead of reading what is written, change the story into something silly. For example, if you're reading the "Three Little Pigs," instead of having a wolf come to the door, make it a gorilla!

5. Pause for a moment after you say the silly part, to see your toddler's reaction. When she says, "No! That's not right!" read it correctly for a few more pages.

6. Then surprise her again with another silly change.

7. Continue making up silly parts for the rest of the story.

Variation: Do the same for a favorite song, changing the words to create a Silly Song, such as "Old MacDonald Had a Car"!

Safety: If your toddler gets upset at the changes, play the game another time.

SMELLY FUN

Your baby is born with a good sense of smell. He can tell mom from dad just by their unique smells, right from birth. By the time he's a toddler, he'll enjoy enriching his sense with a game of Smelly Fun!

Materials:
- Fragrant items for your toddler to smell, such as cologne, toddler food, flower, toddler lotion, clean laundry, scented toy, piece of plastic, bar of soap, and so on
- Paper lunch bags

Learning Skills:	• Cause and effect
	• Classification skills
	• Sensory exploration

What to Do:

1. Collect a variety of fragrant items, as suggested above. Try to choose items familiar to your toddler.

2. Place each item in a separate paper bag and fold over the tops of bags.

3. Set the bags on the floor, and seat your toddler and yourself on the floor next to the bags.

4. Take one bag and open the top.

5. Inhale the contents, to show your toddler how to play, then let him have a whiff, without showing him the contents.

6. Ask him to guess what's inside. Prompt him if he needs help.

7. Open the bag and let your toddler pull out the item to see what it is.

8. Repeat with all the bags.

Variation: Have your toddler smell just food items, such as an orange, a banana, a bread slice, a cookie, some strong cheese, a piece of chocolate, some vegetables, and so on.

Safety: Don't use anything that smells too strong or unpleasant or the game will not be fun.

SNIFF...SNIFF!

S.O.S.

Here's a searching game you can play in the bathtub or outside in the kiddy pool. Watch your toddler as she tries to figure out where the ship has gone!

Materials:
- Bathtub, plastic tub, or kiddy pool
- Water
- Small plastic toys, such as boats
- Washcloths

Learning Skills:	• Fine motor development • Problem solving • Social interaction

What to Do:

1. Fill a tub with warm water.

2. Put your toddler in the water.

3. Set several floating toys in the water, such as small plastic boats.

4. Cover the boats with washcloths.

5. Ask your toddler, "Where did the boats go?" and see if she can find them.

Variation: Instead of using toys that float, use toys that sink and see if your child can find them on the bottom of the tub or pool.

Safety: Watch your toddler around water at all times.

STiCKER SEARCH

In this form of Hide-and-Go-Seek, your toddler searches for stickers instead of people. Use your imagination to hide the stickers in fun places!

Materials:
- Variety of stickers
- Playroom

Learning Skills:	• Gross and fine motor development • Problem solving • Visual tracking and acuity

What to Do:

1. Buy some interesting, self-adhesive stickers.

2. Place the stickers on various items in the playroom, such as furniture, lamps, toys, the floor or walls, shoes, even the dog! Keep all the stickers in plain view.

3. Bring your toddler into the room and tell him to look for the stickers you have hidden.

4. Give him hints if he needs help, using "hot" or "cold" as he gets closer or farther from an item.

5. Have your child stick the stickers to his shirt as he finds them.

Variation: Let your toddler hide the stickers, then you try to find them. Instead of using stickers, use small toys, treats, pictures, or anything else of interest to your toddler.

Safety: Don't place stickers where your child will have to reach, push, pull, crawl, or make any other dangerous effort to reach them. Make sure all stickers are clearly visible, to minimize your toddler's frustration.

STORYBOOK THEATER

If you toddler has a favorite book, turn the make-believe story into a real-live play, with masks, props, and costumes. Watch your toddler's delight as familiar characters leap from the page and onto the stage!

Materials:
- Blanket
- Favorite storybook
- Costume props for whatever characters you choose

Learning Skills:	• Creativity and imagination • Dramatic play • Language and vocabulary development

What to Do:

1. Spread out a blanket in the middle of a room to make a stage.

2. Choose one of your toddler's favorite storybooks, such as *Winnie-the-Pooh* or *Curious George*.

3. Create costume props for the book's characters.

4. Read the story to your toddler.

5. Then get out the costume props and dress yourself and your toddler as the characters.

6. Act out the story together, using the blanket stage.

Variation: Use dolls or puppets to play the parts, instead of yourselves, if you prefer.

Safety: If your toddler gets scared during the dramatic play, remind her it's just make believe. To make the play more fun for her, have her choose the character she wants to act.

174

TiGHTROPE WALK

Your toddler walks easily at this age, but you can challenge him with a game of Tightrope Walk. You try it, too! The game won't be easy, but it will be fun!

Materials:
- Floor space
- Masking tape

Learning Skills:	• Balance and coordination • Eye/foot coordination • Gross motor development

What to Do:

1. Clear the room so you have lots of floor space.

2. Make a line along the floor with masking tape—start with a straight line, then make it twist and bend, and end it with a spiral.

3. Challenge your toddler to a Tightrope Walk. You try it first, by walking on the tape. Try not to step off the tape!

4. Then let your toddler have a turn, and see if he can stay on the tape better than you can.

Variation: Make the tape go all through the house, even over furniture, for a fun obstacle course. Try walking backwards on the tape!

Safety: Don't lead your toddler into any danger- ous areas using the tape. If he has trouble with balance and gets frustrat- ed, line the tape parallel to the wall, so he can use the wall for balance.

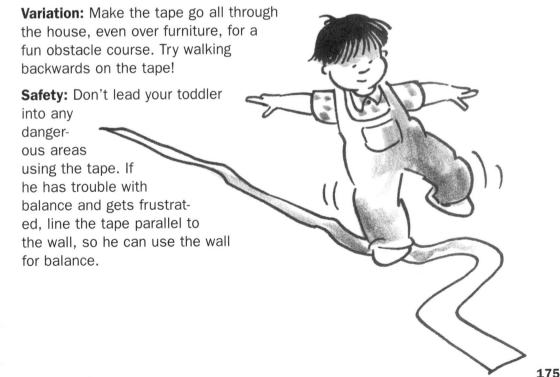

WATER WONDERS

Water offers your growing toddler opportunities for play at every developmental stage. Children never get tired of exploring the mysterious properties of water, so offer your toddler a world of Water Wonders!

Materials:
- Large plastic tub
- Toys to manipulate in the water—plastic measuring cups for pouring; turkey baster for squeezing, filling, and squirting; colander or funnel for sifting or siphoning; straw for blowing; manual egg beater for stirring; ladle for filling and pouring; plastic plates for floating, and so on

Learning Skills:	• Creativity and imagination • Exploration of scientific properties • Fine motor development

What to Do:

1. Place a large plastic tub outside and fill it with lukewarm water.

2. Place various objects, as suggested above, into the tub.

3. Let your toddler explore the water with the help of the various items.

4. After allowing her time to explore the items, demonstrate each object's use, so she has even more options for play.

Variation: Add bubbles to the water for added fun. Play Water Wonder in the bath, if you prefer.

Safety: Never leave your toddler alone during water play.

WHAT HAPPENED?

To increase your toddler's thinking and problem-solving skills, play a game of What Happened? You might be surprised at your toddler's answers.

Materials:

- Pictures showing a dramatic or thought-provoking situation, such as a cat climbing a wall, a toddler crying, a spilled drink, a surprised child, a broken toy, an eaten pizza, and so on
- Scissors
- Construction paper
- Glue

Learning Skills:	• Cognitive/thinking skills • Language development • Problem solving • Social interaction

What to Do:

1. Find some magazine pictures that show a dramatic or thought-provoking situation, such as those described above.

2. Cut out the pictures and glue them onto sheets of construction paper to make them easy to handle and examine.

3. Sit on the floor with your toddler and hold up one of the pictures.

4. Ask your toddler, "What happened?" As you ask, make a puzzled-looking face and shrug your shoulders.

5. Let your toddler have some time to think and come up with an answer. If he needs help, give him clues.

6. When he figures out the problem, go on to the next picture.

Variation: After your toddler identifies the problem, ask him to help you solve it. For example, if a cat is stuck in a tree, say, "What should we do?"

Safety: Don't use any pictures that are too complicated or that may upset your toddler. Keep the game light and fun.

INDEX

Also from Meadowbrook Press

✦ Busy Books

The Toddler's Busy Book and *The Preschooler's Busy Book* each contains 365 activities (one for each day of the year) for your children using items found around the home. The books offer parents and child-care providers fun reading, math, and science activities that will stimulate a child's natural curiosity. They also provide great activities for indoor play during even the longest stretches of bad weather! Both show you how to save money by making your own paints, play dough, craft clays, glue, paste, and other arts-and-crafts supplies.

✦ Feed Me! I'm Yours

Parents love this easy-to-use, economical guide to making baby food at home. More than 200 recipes cover everything a parent needs to know about teething foods, nutritious snacks, and quick, pleasing lunches.

✦ Play and Learn

Baby Play and Learn and *Preschooler Play and Learn*, from child-development expert Penny Warner, offer ideas for games and activities that will provide hours of developmental learning opportunities and fun for young children and babies. Each book contains bulleted lists of skills your child will learn through play activities, step-by-step instructions, and illustrations.

✦ When You Were a Baby

This one-of-a-kind board book is the only baby record book designed with a die-cut hole that enables parents to prominently feature baby's photograph on every page, with colorful illustrations showing such personal landmarks as birth, crawling, first bath, first word, first birthday, and more. The fun illustrations capture each milestone in a warm yet humorous way.

✦ When You Were One

Personalize landmark events in your child's early life such as saying the first sentence, drawing the first picture, going down a slide, and much more. This board book with a die-cut hole allows you to display a photo of your child in each colorful illustration. With fill-in-the-blank sections, parents can record all the details of their one-year-old's milestones and memorable moments.

**We offer many more titles written to delight, inform, and entertain.
To order books with a credit card or browse our full
selection of titles, visit our web site at:**

www.meadowbrookpress.com

or call toll-free to place an order, request a free catalog, or ask a question:

1-800-338-2232

Meadowbrook Press • 5451 Smetana Drive • Minnetonka, MN • 55343